MW00532807

YOU
ARE
WHERE
YOU
GO

Never stop exploring
the world and yourself!

♡ Caitlyn Lubas

YOU ARE WHERE YOU GO

A Traveler's Coming of Age Journey through
70 Countries and 7 Continents During College

CAITLYN LUBAS

"The shortest path to oneself leads around the world."

—Hermann von Keyserling, German philosopher
The Travel Diary of a Philosopher

Charleston, SC
www.PalmettoPublishing.com

You Are Where You Go:
A Traveler's Coming of Age Journey Through
70 Countries and 7 Continents During College

Copyright © 2021 by Caitlyn Lubas

First Edition

Hardcover: 978-1-63837-542-5
Paperback: 978-1-63837-543-2
eBook: 978-1-63837-544-9

Table of Contents

Author's Note:
An Introduction to My
3 Years of Transformative Travel

"Wherever you go becomes a part of you somehow."

—Anita Desai

I sat cross-legged on the uneven dirt in the rural village of Woadze Tsatoe in eastern Ghana, listening to the chirps of crickets float across the humid evening air as the moonlight illuminated the faces of my peers who had transformed from classmates to volunteer-mates to lifelong friends. Stars twinkled above our heads as we shared reflections about how Ghana had become a part of all of us through the eye-opening experiences of the past week.

Our hearts and minds would forever be filled with scenes from the village of Woadze Tsatoe: The musical laughter from the schoolchildren as they played Duck Duck Goose with us. The vibrant rainbow of batik fabric that we hand-printed ourselves. The stillness of Lake Volta during morning fishing boat rides. The pulsing energy of the drums and gourd-instruments that started a village dance party. The warmth and generosity of our host families welcoming us into their homes with the universal language of a smile.

My best friend Amy sighed and leaned her head back. We projected our memories from the past few days onto the vast expanse of twinkling stars above us. "Everywhere you go becomes part of you," she whispered. "Even though we came on this trip hoping to make an impact on the local villagers, the trip ended up making more of an impact on *us*."

Each of us chooses what we prioritize in life. The places we select to visit and the frequency at which we decide to travel say a lot about who we are as people and what we value.

By the age of 18, I had been to various "typical" tourist destinations: Rome, Paris, London, Amsterdam, Bangkok, and the Philippines (my mother's homeland). I took the first "unconventional" trip of my life when I traveled to Ghana with a group of peers and professors from my university's social entrepreneurship class for my first spring break during college. There, I found myself waking up under a mosquito net in a mud hut in a rural village rather than waking up hungover at a beach or in a foreign city. Not your typical spring break, by any means.

Ghana changed me in every way. Physically, my sunburned skin was dotted with mosquito bites. Emotionally, my heart felt fuller and more connected to others than it ever had. Mentally, my head was now crowded with unshakeable new perspectives that would ground me in a new baseline of what is "normal."

Experiencing life in a different corner of the world had contrasting effects of feeling vastly different, yet eerily familiar. I reveled in the realization that the same threads of the human experience connect us all in a global tapestry, no matter our physical location.

I could now associate specific names, faces, foods, sights, and sounds with a country that my mind had previously shrouded in mere assumptions. I thought about all the other countries in the world I had yet to visit. Where else did my mental map of the globe currently have a foggy question mark rather than colorful memories, interesting facts, and friendly faces? I wanted to discover them all, to bring every country out of the shadows, and integrate everywhere into the mosaic of places that make me who I am.

Luckily, this Ghana trip took place during my first year of university, and I realized I had time. A beautiful buffer of three more years stood between my 18-year-old self and the "real world" after graduation. When I initially sought out prospective colleges during high school, I prioritized any school that would offer unique opportunities to live in another country. I remembered hearing adults say that their only regret in life was that they wished they had traveled more, and I refused to have that regret.

On that flight home from Ghana in March 2017, my insatiable curiosity about the world inspired me to set a goal of visiting all seven continents and as many countries as possible during my three remaining years of college.

I had been told for years that post-graduate life entailed working... and working... and working... until that sweet reward of retirement. I had read books like *Eat, Pray, Love* where victims of loss and wanderlust transformed a midlife crisis into a trip around the globe. I had followed travel influencers and nomadic bloggers who swapped out a traditional career for a life on the move. According to society, only after a midlife crisis, career change, or forty years of working could you finally start living the exciting life you always imagined for yourself.

But what if I didn't want to wait until retirement, or a midlife crisis? What if I still cared about starting a career and making a positive impact on the world? How could I make travel a part of my everyday life, at the ripe age of 18?

I decided that a fun life of travel and conventional "success" did not have to be mutually exclusive. I adopted a "yes, and" mentality, throwing my "no, but" excuses out the window.

People often think they can't find the time, or the money, or the courage to get out and see the world, but the key to being able to travel is simply adopting the right mindset. Growing up, my dad always told me, "Once you put your mind to something, there's nothing you can't do." If you make a steadfast commitment to adjust your mindset, ruthlessly prioritize, and make necessary sacrifices, then yes, you can travel the world. And yes, you can still develop a career, relationships, funds, or anything else that you might initially perceive as a roadblock to travel.

People often remark, "You're so lucky," when they hear about my travel experiences. It's not about being lucky; it's about having the right attitude and committing to a plan of action.

I stopped saying, "I can't wait to travel the world," and decided that indeed, *I could not wait.* I shifted my goals and immediately started seeking out and saying yes to every opportunity to get out there and explore the world. After a whirlwind three years of flinging myself across the globe multiple times over, I emerged as a 21-year-old who has visited 70 countries across 7 continents during college.

Throughout my nomadic college journey, I lived and learned in the unique cultural contexts of Ghana, Italy, Israel, Singapore, the United Arab Emirates, and Peru, along with New York City—my home base. I did this through a mix of full semesters abroad and short-term international immersion courses and fellowships over winter and spring break. Hard work and dedication enabled me to graduate a semester early to embark on a post-graduation trip with the goal of visiting all seven continents in seven months, before COVID-19 had other plans for the world and me.

I look back at each experience abroad as a key chapter in my coming-of-age story. Replace the sound of turning the page of a book with the sound of a jet taking off, and you start to get a clear picture of how I see chapters of my life, and the stages of my personal growth, spread out across the world.

I believe that life begins outside your comfort zone, and by putting myself in unfamiliar situations abroad, often without the safety net of my close friends, I was able to experience incredible personal growth. The sometimes grueling behind-the-scenes of contorting myself into tight budget airline seats, waking up delirious after a night on an overnight bus, coexisting with over a dozen other strangers in a hostel dorm, and scarfing down street food without knowing how it may affect my stomach were all worth it for the ultimate highs of seeing new places for the first time and acquiring a clearer view of the world.

Before travel, my worldview was like an old radio tuned into a channel that was only producing static—uninformed and lacking any key message. Each unique experience abroad allowed me to tune into a clearer signal of what the world is really like—dynamic, vibrant, and enlightening.

I don't see travel as a mechanism for checking off a list of countries. To me, traveling is gifting yourself the opportunity to dive into a sea of new experiences and perspectives, to morph into a sponge and soak up all the world has to offer, and then come home, wring yourself out, and discover how your travel has shaped you. Visiting Antarctica, getting stitches after a motorbike accident in rural

Vietnam, camping on an overland safari for six weeks straight, and spending every weekend in a different country for ten months of my life are all unique examples of adventures abroad that have molded me into the person I am today.

It is nearly impossible to describe all the impactful experiences from over seventy countries I've been lucky enough to experience. Rather than a comprehensive retelling of every place and experience, this book shares with you the key perspective-shifting moments from my travels: vivid immersions into uncommon corners of the world coupled with personal reflections about many of life's greatest lessons that are each tied to a significant place. To help anyone execute life-changing trips of their own, I'll also share a breakdown of considerations for how to plan trips like the ones I share in this book.

To leave you with a reader's compass: the chapters are in chronological order of my personal journey, but each is a self-contained story that can be read individually, and out of order. Therefore, I invite you to explore the book in whole or in part, at random or in order, according to whatever country or lesson piques your interest. My years of travel during college have been nomadic and unpredictable, and so too can your reading style.

For the students staring down the next few years before adulthood: I hope this book inspires you to prioritize travel in your college years by adopting that "yes, and" mentality that unlocks opportunity and personal growth.

For the travel lovers: I hope this book sparks a moment of reminiscence about your own unique experiences where you explored a deeper level of yourself while exploring the world.

For the travel curious: I hope these stories transport you to distant corners of the globe so you can gain the key takeaways even if you aren't yet ready to leave the comfort of your own home.

For my future self: I hope this time capsule of your young adult thoughts, experiences, and perspectives always serves as a humble reminder that you are where you go.

The Decision: Prioritizing Travel

"Making a decision was only the beginning of things. When someone makes a decision, he is really diving into a strong current that will carry him to places he had never dreamed of when he first made the decision."

—Paulo Coelho, *The Alchemist*

While writing this book, whenever I met someone new and told them I was writing about my experiences traveling to 70 countries and 7 continents at the age of 21, their first question was almost always the same—*How?!*

How did you manage to fit that into your schedule? How did you finance these travels? How did you find the courage to travel solo or with strangers? How did you have the energy to travel so frequently?

Before getting into specific stories from my college-student journey around the world, I'll share some tactical advice for how to make your travel dreams a reality.

Make the Choice

Prioritizing travel is a choice that anyone can make, but not everyone does.

We all make choices every day that enable us to achieve the things that we want most in life. Some people prioritize seeking career success and dedicate the majority of their free time and energy towards optimizing for the next step in their professional development. Others may prioritize finding love or investing in their friendships by making choices that best position themselves for stability in these personal relationships.

In an empanada-making class I took in Argentina, I met a well-traveled, curly-haired girl around my age whose spunky attitude and wise words will always stick with me. As we swapped travel stories and folded dough into half-moon formations, she philosophized, "Most people aren't too poor to travel. They're just either too lazy to do things that will help them save money, or too focused on the wrong things in life."

At first, I thought her conclusion reeked of privilege. Surely some people can't afford to travel, no matter what, because they are unfortunately preoccupied with making ends meet. Some people are truly in survival mode. And before you can focus on thriving, you must be at least surviving.

But the more I thought about her perspective, the more I realized that for the majority of people, her words do ring true.

Many of us choose to eat out. We take Ubers instead of walking. We blow money on alcohol, going out, and frivolous one-time purchases that give us the temporary dopamine hits our brains crave. We buy unnecessary five-dollar lattes. We engage in retail therapy.

All of these decisions can bring joy in the moment, but they can certainly be sacrificed. If you start evaluating your spending decisions in relation to the cost of a flight, or the cost of lodging and meals in a foreign country, you can clearly see the trade-offs. One rush-hour Uber downtown when you're too lazy to walk, or a budget airline ticket that will transport you to a new city or country?

The choice is yours.

Once you've decided that travel is your priority, you realize that dozens of nights out and aesthetic morning coffees aren't in line with your focus. You hone in on making those necessary monetary or time-commitment trade-offs that help you get closer to your goal. You start cooking rather than ordering delivery, trading leisure time for a side hustle that brings in extra income, planning out necessary purchases instead of impulse buying, and making decisions such that your money and time—two of your most finite resources—are allocated in line with your priority of travel.

Determine Your *Why*

In order to shift travel into that number-one slot on your list of priorities, contemplate your *Why*. Ask yourself, what is the reason you want to travel? Do you want to learn about new ways of life in different corners of the world? Do you want to experience new foods and new cultures? Do you want to challenge yourself in a new environment and learn more about the natural world? Would you rather see a place with your own eyes than hear about it a hundred times from friends or in the media? Keep that purpose top of mind.

If you make a steadfast decision that you want to travel the world, everything else can find a way to work and fit in around that priority. It's all about setting that intention and making necessary adjustments, sacrifices, and mental shifts to go from travel aspirations in your head to plane tickets in your hand.

For me, travel was the thing that I prioritized above all else. I've been inspired to travel ever since I was a little girl, sitting on my Grandpa Joe's lap while listening to stories of his international explorations. My grandpa spent decades working for a travel agency and eventually owned his own tour company, which enabled him to bring my dad to many exotic places as a child. When I grew up hearing stories of my dad eating monkey brain at a bazaar in Marrakech and exploring his grandparents' homeland of Poland in the 1980s before the fall of communism, this itch to explore the world transferred to me.

Hearing firsthand accounts from someone as close to me as my dad made the idea of travel seem real. Walking through exotic scenery and experiencing foreign flavors on your tongue weren't just for rich people in movies or celebrities on social media. Having my dad and grandpa as real-life reference points solidified the idea in my young, malleable brain that travel could be for anyone. I hope that I can be that real-life reference point for readers like you—travel is for you, and is within your means!

My mom also served as a fair share of travel inspiration herself, since she was born and raised halfway across the globe in the Philippines before immigrating to the United States with the Filipino half of my family during her early teenage years.

Following these bits of travel inspiration from my childhood, I found my motivation for travel around that awkward age of 13 when you're trying to figure out who you are and where you fit into the world.

At an early age, I joined global social media sites like Twitter for the first time, which helped me connect with an international network of fellow music-loving teenagers (what we now call *stan* Twitter, in Internet speak). The ability to talk to people from different countries and learn so much about other cultures from real people rather than from books or videos lit up my imagination.

I formed strong bonds with online friends around the world who I couldn't wait to meet one day by traveling to their home countries. At a relatively young age, I grew comfortable interacting with strangers from different places and became insatiably curious about other customs, perspectives, and nuances of language and humor.

Your inspiration and motivation to travel may differ from mine. But whatever your *Why*—find it, and focus on it.

Manifest Your How

The *How* that determines your ability to travel may play out in different ways, too.

If you wanted to follow in my footsteps exactly, I would transparently say that attending a university that emphasizes studying abroad is a key factor in traveling as much as possible during college. I chose New York University.

NYU sends nearly half of its students abroad during their college careers—more than any other American college or university. I also strategically chose to major in Global Business. This academic path aligned with my personal interest in how companies cater their products and services to different cultural preferences and regional intricacies. Most importantly, this course of study offered the greatest opportunities to take experiential learning courses abroad that were specifically crafted for this major.

I realize that advising people to mimic my exact college journey is not very actionable advice. Creating a strategic life trajectory to prioritize travel may happen during a high schooler's college application phase, like it did for me, but this is by no means a requirement. Studying Global Business and adopting an internationally focused academic path is how I made travel fit into my life, but making travel a priority can take many different forms.

There are a few key tips I'd keep in mind when you're figuring out your own way of manifesting how you'll focus on travel in your life:

Tip #1: Prepare to Make Social and Financial Sacrifices

First, be in the mindset to make sacrifices, if necessary, that are both social and financial.

To gain my ability to travel, I learned to operate on six hours of sleep or less as I worked multiple jobs at once, year-round, for four years straight, on top of being a full-time student. I lived within my means and never went into debt or over-spent on credit cards.

I never indulged in renting an apartment for blissful summers of living with friends in New York City. Instead, I commuted to my jobs in the city on crowded, smelly New Jersey Transit buses for over two hours a day from my small suburban family home.

I never had a steady romantic relationship throughout college because I was usually only in one place for less than six months at a time.

I never signed a lease, subjecting my nomadic life to the whims of whatever sublet happened to be cheap and available. The practice of buying furniture for an apartment and having a sense of permanent place is foreign to me. The call of the new and novel, the chase of a change of scenery, and the euphoria of experiencing a new place for the first time all feel more familiar to me than the stagnancy of a single place called home.

I was so enthusiastic about my priority of traveling that my *How*—which involved social sacrifice and strategic financial decisions—was worth it in the long run, no matter how seemingly undesirable at the time.

In addition to the sacrifices I made back home, I learned how to stretch my dollars as much as possible when actually on the road. Staying in hotels or flying anything fancier than basic economy class became an unfamiliar concept. In some countries, it can cost as little as $5 a day for a bed in a hostel and local street food. Budget airlines with trans-European flights for as little as 99 cents and discount overnight buses with prices in the single digits became my best friends. Roughing it with mediocre transportation and shoestring budget accommodation was always worth it for the richness of my experiences in a new country.

Though some may think I've missed out on certain parts of life, I don't regret my choices in the slightest because they enabled me to make my dreams of living and exploring abroad a reality.

Tip #2: Get Over Your FOMO

A lot of students choose not to study abroad because they don't want to miss out on the typical college experience, surrounded by their friends and the comforts of campus life. I like to think of *FOMO* not in terms of fear of missing out on what's happening at home with my friends, but fear of missing out *on life.*

If I stayed home and didn't travel, there are endless combinations of experiences, people, and slices of life abroad that I would have missed out on. To me, the people who choose to stay at home are the ones missing out.

It's all about shifting your perspective to help motivate yourself to silence the little voice inside that may be telling you to not book that plane ticket, or to not enroll in that program abroad, out of fear.

Forcing yourself to meet new people and live in a new place while the people you love back home live their normal lives can be scary, no doubt. But you'll grow, learn, and come back home with new friends, experiences, and perspectives that build upon what you had before you left home. Going abroad is an additive life decision, not one that involves missing out.

Tip #3: Do the Thing Your Future Self Will Thank You For

My *Why* for travel, especially during college, also stems from a strong belief that travel is more beneficial now than later. Travel while you're young because you'll never be younger than you are today. You can always find ways to make more money, but no one yet has figured out how to add more time to your life.

There's a reason that people choose to go to school when they are young. Getting an education serves as a solid foundation for you to make consequential decisions later in life based on that foundational knowledge.

Travel is no different—you stand to benefit most from acquiring diverse global perspectives when you are still at a formative stage in life. By choosing to travel at the earliest possible opportunity, your opinions and viewpoints are most malleable and you have the opportunity to develop decision-making processes and core values at an early age that will impact the rest of your life.

If I didn't go abroad during college and learn how to adjust to a new environment while forming new social circles, it's likely that I would not openly embrace the opportunity to move to a new city after graduation and would not have such a nomadic spirit.

If I didn't travel often and for long lengths of time, I would probably be a lot more materialistic. Instead of acquiring physical things, I now prioritize acquiring experiences. I know I can get by for months with just the essentials that fit in a backpack.

If I didn't have experience living all over the world, I may not have structured my career path to specifically include opportunities to travel. One of the reasons I was initially drawn to working for a technology company like Instagram as my first job out of college is because social media is inherently global and helps connect people all around the world.

Without the knowledge and perspectives gained from traveling, I would not have evolved into this new version of myself that I am today. I often look back and thank my 18-year-old self for setting out on this path of ruthlessly prioritizing travel above all else. Will you be able to look back and thank your younger self? If that's not currently the case, make some changes to ensure your future self thanks you.

Tip #4: Choose Something Comfortable, Then Expand Your Horizons

Choosing to travel does not necessarily mean diving off the deep end and catapulting yourself out of your comfort zone. You can choose to slowly increase your radius of comfort trip by trip, until your comfort zone expands and encompasses the entire world.

I first studied abroad in Europe where most people are "Westernized" and not extremely dissimilar from what I was used to in the United States, save for some language barriers and varying cultural norms.

Then, I did an exchange semester in Singapore where the language was still primarily English but I was in close proximity to very new and very distinct cultures. After growing comfortable with the uncomfortable, I pushed myself to my limits through more adventurous travel that forced me to confront new cultures and environments. Immersing myself in the Islamic world in the United Arab Emirates, visiting Antarctica, trekking Patagonia, and camping for weeks on an African safari are just a few examples that helped me expand my comfort zone to every corner of this earth.

These experiences all made me realize that what I previously considered my "limit" was not actually a limit at all. Challenging myself through these travels and experiences made me realize I have more capacity for growth and endurance than previously realized.

Traveling to new places can transform you into someone who may seem like a stranger to your former self. Travel can show you how small you are in the grand scheme of things, and this realization makes the world seem bigger and more inspiring by contrast. All it takes is a step outside of your comfort zone.

Tip #5: Travel with Intention

When thinking about travel, it's easy to get caught up in a whirlwind of fanciful aspects like envisioning the stunning Instagram photos you'll take, drooling at the thought of tasting exotic foods for the first time, and escaping from the drudgery of day-to-day life into a world that's temporarily different and endlessly stimulating.

But before getting caught up with exactly where to travel, when is the best season to go, or what to do first in a new city, I advise you to hone in on your intention for traveling.

What do you wish to achieve through travel? For me, the world is not a checklist of places to be seen, but rather a treasure trove of perspectives to be collected and experienced.

Travel because you can collect experiences. Travel because no one can ever take away your memories. No natural disaster can ever destroy the moments that you've enjoyed in your life. Some people prioritize buying things and accumulating possessions, but for me, travel is an immaterial possession that no one can value as much as you.

I encourage you to travel with the motive to undertake not just a physical journey, but also a mental and emotional one. As our bodies move through new countries, taste new foods, and greet new people, our minds move through new customs, social norms, and languages that cover as much mental ground as our feet do across the physical earth.

Instead of a to-do list or a to-see list, make a to-be list. When you focus your travels around the emotions and states of mind you want to embody, rather than just the activities or attractions you want to do or see, you will be more fulfilled in your travels.

When the world begins to feel borderless, the walls between the disparate parts of yourself also begin to crumble. Each stamp in your passport is a permission slip to overcome a barrier within yourself, to discover an uncharted facet of your personality while exploring uncharted new locations.

We are all part of a global interconnected puzzle, and each trip we take shakes us the tiniest bit closer into our rightful place to complete that puzzle, and to complete ourselves.

Connecting with as many places and people as possible is the journey toward completing the puzzle within yourself.

When you decide to travel, you decide to change your life. In a tangible way, you are changing your physical location by displacing yourself from the comforts of home and willingly injecting the unfamiliar into your life. In a more amorphous way, you are opening your mind to new cultures, ideas, and perspectives perhaps never previously considered.

Travel because you alone have the power to unlock new aspects of your personality and expand your worldview, as long as you choose to travel with the intention of learning and growing.

Tip #6: Take Advantage of Fresh Starts

For most people, starting your first year of college is the beginning of a brand-new chapter. You have the next four years laid out in front of you, often in a completely new city and detached from any old version of yourself you might have formed in high school.

A fresh, blank canvas to kick off a new chapter of life is invigorating. Having the opportunity to meet new people and introduce yourself for the first time gives you the chance to redefine yourself and realign your values. You get to ask yourself, "Am I the person I want to be?" and if not, then you can use this new beginning to put yourself on the right path towards being that person.

I often felt restricted by the reputation I had developed for myself in high school. As the valedictorian who graduated at the top of my class, I was mainly known for being "the smart girl." I was usually pretty quiet, and probably wouldn't be the first person you'd ask to join you on a wild night out or risk-taking adventure.

But in college, the thought of being a stranger to everyone around me was endlessly exciting as I stepped out of my dorm on Fifth Avenue in the heart of New York City each morning. No one knew me here! I had no preconceived notions holding me back! I was free to let myself become that person that I wanted to be: the type of person who would hit the ground running in the greatest city in the world and maximize every opportunity presented to her.

Starting college in New York City allowed me to become the version of myself that best fit my new location. I became a product of the city I lived, learned, worked, loved, cried, and laughed in.

But my process of reinvention and letting every place become part of me didn't stop there. When I embarked on my class trip to Ghana as a college freshman, I explored new facets of myself and adopted social impact as a core professional value.

When I studied and lived abroad for the first time in Florence, I started becoming known as "that girl who travels every weekend" as I relentlessly explored the far reaches of Europe on my long weekends.

During a coding and entrepreneurship fellowship in Tel Aviv, I was no longer a big fish in a small pond for the first time, and learned how to deal with imposter syndrome. I lost myself, then found myself again on the other side of my pride.

In Singapore, as an exchange student, far away from any friends or fellow NYU students, I experienced what it was like to be the only American in the room for the first time in my life. I reinvented myself once again, manifesting the effusive, bubbly personality that I had admired in others back home in New York.

Your identity is usually a product of external factors like where you work, where you grew up, or where you went to school. When you travel, you get to create your own identity and tell new people what you care about. You redefine yourself in the context of a new country and in the eyes of new friends who have no preconceived notions of who you are or what you're like. By choosing to share, or not share, specific things about yourself, you create your own sense of self in every new place you visit and with every new person you meet.

Each trip that dropped me in a new location and a new social context gave me that gift of a fresh start. I will always relish an opportunity to take in a new environment, let it shape me, and emerge as a new version of myself. These experiences, many of which you'll read about in this book, are a testament to the fact that you are where you go.

Italy: A First Taste of Life Abroad

"For us to go to Italy and to penetrate into Italy is like a most fascinating act of self-discovery."

—D. H. Lawrence

"Buongiorno! We are now beginning our descent into the city of Florence. Please fasten your seatbelts and make sure your seat backs and tray tables are in their full upright positions."

The smooth feminine voice tinged with an Italian accent floated through the airplane cabin, causing the sense of unease in my stomach to kick into overdrive. The plane turbulence had long subsided. Now, pure nervousness took its place.

"This is it, the beginning of a whole new chapter," I told myself. "Get excited! Living in Italy is a dream come true!"

I tried to coax myself into believing this, but couldn't ignore the tension devouring my stomach faster than I had hoped to devour a creamy scoop of gelato immediately upon landing.

What if I wasn't able to make new friends to travel with? What if I got lost and my limited Italian-language skills weren't sufficient to ask for help? What if everyone back home in New York moved on with their lives and made new friends while I was thousands of miles away exploring Europe?

It was only my second year of college, and I had been lucky enough to solidify a dependable group of friends by the end of the previous semester—a feat that, at a school like New York University that happened to be in the middle of a bustling city without any centralized campus, was an accomplishment in itself.

Did I really want to have to basically go through freshman year all over again? I shuddered thinking about having to introduce myself to new people and constantly "put myself out there" to cross paths with friends who could become potential new travel buddies.

The six-hour time difference between Italy and all of my family and friends back in New York didn't help with my apprehension. I was already beginning to do mental math every time I looked at the clock—*ok, so if it's 10 a.m. here, it's 4 a.m. back home...*—to level my expectations about when I could expect messages and replies throughout the day.

Although I was excited to embrace the independence of living by myself in a foreign country, a slight fear lurked in the back of my mind about what would happen in case anything were to ever go wrong while I was thousands of miles away from my parents who would normally do anything in their power to protect and help me.

Before starting my first semester abroad, I had been to Italy a few times because my dad's half-brother is Italian and lives in a Tuscan beach town. It had always been a bit confusing for me to say I have family from Italy even though zero percent of my DNA is of Italian descent—my Polish grandfather had first married, then divorced, an Italian woman before marrying my actual grandmother, who was also Polish.

But choosing to spend a semester in the "cradle of the Renaissance" full of art at every corner, with the crown jewel of the *Duomo* merely steps away from my apartment, felt right. Maybe it was somewhere in my DNA not to be ethnically Italian, but to become temporarily Italian and let this country shape me in some small way.

The cabin loudspeaker dinged to indicate our ability to remove our seatbelts and the Italian man beside me on the flight gave me a smile, the kind that strangers do when they can't speak your language but want to communicate an aura of friendliness.

"Andiamo!" he joyfully quipped.

"Let's go, indeed," I whispered to myself as I prepared to dive right into this new beginning in a new country, no matter what struggles might lie ahead.

After a month, Florence, which once felt so foreign, was as familiar as my hometown.

My New York City walking pace that used to accelerate me down 15 city blocks in the span of 15 minutes had given way to the slower pace of Tuscany. I learned the art of the casual stroll, giving me the chance to peer into the gelato shops with their rainbows of creamy goodness stacked high behind glass cases, to catch a whiff of freshly baked pizza as I sauntered through the cobblestone Florentine streets, to stop and hum along with the Italian street musicians who made me feel as if I were starring in my own musical when I was simply en route to the grocery store.

Until my semester in Florence, all of my education had taken place in American classrooms. But here in Florence, I ambled along the streets where everyone around me spoke Italian, looked Italian, and acted Italian. *This* was the classroom. My environment could teach me more than a book about Italy ever could.

By the end of just one month, I couldn't remember the last time I needed to open Google Maps to navigate. The city's meandering streets had already etched themselves into my mind:

- The daily 33-minute uphill walk to reach the olive-tree-lined estate, *Villa La Pietra*, that housed my college classes;

- The quick jaunt down the street to grab a pistachio creme-filled *cannolo* while soaking in the energy of swarms of tourists awaiting their chance to gaze up at the classical paintings adorning the ceilings of the *Duomo*;

- The 15-minute stroll across the medieval bridges that spanned the Arno River to reach *Gusta Pizza*, the pizzeria where you could get an entire pizza for merely a few euros, and even get it made in the shape of a heart, if the chefs thought you were cute;

- The well-traveled 30-minute (or 25-, if speed-walking in a time crunch) route from my apartment to the *Santa Maria Novella* station: the origin of each weekend trip that either started with a whistle of a train on its way to a nearby airport or the hum of an idling neon green FlixBus about to depart for a budget-friendly overnight journey.

I knew this new city like the back of my hand and felt a sense of home I had previously only felt in America. A few key events completed my transition from tourist to local.

Late one night, well past midnight, even as it started to drizzle, my apartment-mates and I wandered the cobblestone streets and let our noses lead the way towards a famous secret bakery. A beacon of light streaming out of an unmarked building verified the source of the heavenly smell—flaky Nutella croissants generously coated in powdered sugar, for just a euro each! As we indulged ourselves under the yellow glow of the streetlamp, the Nutella melted in our mouths and this moment melted our hearts with love for the hidden gems of Florence.

I became friendly with Fernando, the barista at the cafe inside the Italian villa housing my classrooms. I developed a routine of arriving about 30 minutes early for my 9 a.m. class in order to review my Italian language readings, while sipping a perfect cup of espresso and enjoying a fresh croissant—all for one euro and forty cents. After a few weeks of establishing this routine, I was ready with the exact change as Fernando greeted me each day with a *Buongiorno* and a smile, whipping up my standard order before I even needed to say it: *Caffè latte e un cornetto, per favore.* A barista in Italy knew me as a regular! What could be more Italian than that?

These serendipitous moments of local life, brick by brick, formed the foundation for my feeling of belonging in this new country.

On my way home to my apartment every day, I passed the gallery that housed Michelangelo's famous statue of David and marveled at the fact such a masterpiece of Renaissance art could ever be something I just casually strolled past.

At the end of my street, there were always crowds of tourists gawking at the *Duomo*'s façade of pink, green, and white marble. I smiled secretly to myself because I knew that I was no longer one of those tourists.

I was a local, a *Fiorentina*, at least for the next few months.

I started off knowing only key phrases, like *Ciao!* (mysteriously, both goodbye and hello); *Posso avere una bottiglia d'acqua?* (a necessity in a country that didn't automatically serve every meal with a complimentary glass of water as they did back home); and *Via Ricasoli trentotto* (my address). To this day, the only Italian number I remember without fail is 38, because it was my apartment building number.

But through my thrice-weekly Italian classes, my knowledge grew to the point where I was giving presentations entirely in Italian about where I had traveled the previous weekend. Learning a new language was always fun for me, but being able to put ideas into words that fit the cadence and rhythm of the country I was living in felt like the stable foundation I needed to develop my sense of home.

At the beginning, when I woke up, walked outside, and heard a language that didn't process in my brain, it felt like looking at an inverted video of myself—simultaneously familiar, yet foreign. I could understand the emotion and the intonation but not the content or the message. I could tell when someone was asking a question, but not what that question was.

In a touristy city like Florence, English was widely spoken and understood. Even when I attempted to practice my newly minted language skills by ordering my dinner in Italian, the waitress would often take one look at me, deduce that my Asian features and American dress proved I was not a local, and simply answer back in English to save us both the trouble.

Nevertheless, I started finding joy in picking up vocabulary words here and there in conversations that echoed down the hallways or floated on the breeze through my apartment window up from the bustling streets below.

By the end of the semester, when my Italian *professoressa* called me her favorite student and invited me to stay with her at her home anytime I returned to Florence in the future, I felt the warmth of hospitality that only comes from genuine local connections forged through assimilating and learning the local language.

The warmth of the Italian sun chased dribbles of my last scoop of gelato down the side of its cone as I looked out over the city of Florence. From my vantage point, perched atop a hill at *Piazzale Michelangelo*, my eyes soaked in a panorama of the city's terracotta roofed, yellow stucco buildings overshadowed by the iconic cathedral dome and the Tuscan hills in the distance.

"I never thought I would say this, but I can't even look at another scoop of gelato right now." I let out an exasperated sigh and clutched my stomach.

"Ugh, I feel you. Consuming 21 cups of gelato in the span of a few hours is pushing the limits of the human body," affirmed my friend Sebastian.

That September afternoon, mere weeks into our semester abroad in Florence, Sebastian and I had attended The Gelato Festival. The greatest gelato makers from all around Europe had descended upon the birthplace of the Italian Renaissance to compete for votes that determine the best gelato flavor. In order to accurately cast a vote as an attendee, you were required to taste all the flavors, and never had I ever been so excited to put my love for ice cream to good use.

Creamy *fior di latte*, tangy strawberry with balsamic, rich chocolate Nutella, and even an unexpected frozen version of *bruschetta:* tomato-flavored gelato served on bread and topped with olive oil. A seemingly endless stream of unique flavor combinations dazzled my taste buds one by one.

However, as we neared the end of our sampling route and started to lose count if we were on scoop 15 or 19, the initial joy of trying a new gelato flavor had worn off. Each flavor was so delicious and unique that it was hard to even compare them all. Asking me to pick a favorite was an impossible assignment.

We trudged toward the finish line and plopped ourselves down on the ledge overlooking the view of the city. Nearly two dozen scoops of gelato later, our tongues were overstimulated and our bodies were exhausted.

Little did I know, that Gelato Festival experience of squeezing 21 gelato flavor tastings into a single afternoon would turn out to be an accurate representation of the remainder of my semester abroad, as I proceeded to spend the next four months on a mission to get a taste for as many different European countries as possible.

Weeks had passed by in a blur of lectures accented in Italian (it's *in-VEN-tor-y*, not *in-ven-TOR-y*, according to Professor Fabio), local dishes that would forever appear in my dreams (three-cheese truffle gnocchi from *Osteria Santo Spirito*, I'm looking at you), and endless trips to the train and bus terminal.

Though many people travel and study abroad in order to escape routine, my life fell into a new type of routine: Attend classes. Eat pasta. Do homework while listening to travel podcasts for inspiration. Roll clothes, pack backpack. Board plane. Wake up in a new country. See sights, eat local food, pass out from exhaustion in cramped Airbnb or hostel. Cram in one last reading or study session on the flight home. Repeat, week after week after week, but always with a smile on my face. This was the type of routine that brought endless joy, not daily monotony.

In the midst of this weekly travel routine, there was a lot of chaos: wiping sweat off my brow after sprinting through airport terminals to catch tightly timed connecting flights, stumbling through sleep deprivation in new cities after foolishly taking overnight buses two nights in a row, and sneaking in through the back entrances of Airbnbs for which my friends and I definitely exceeded the capacity dictated by the host.

As a novice traveler during these first few months abroad, I hadn't known any better. But I soon appreciated the fact that each travel mishap was both a learning opportunity and a funny story to tell.

After spending every single weekend in a different European country, I looked back at the 21 countries I'd visited and, just like that afternoon overlooking the city of Florence while my stomach threatened to explode, I felt satisfied, overwhelmed, and just a bit in awe of what I had actually been able to experience in such a short amount of time. Most importantly, I was able to look back and understand that the low points where I felt I exceeded my limits were some of the most pivotal parts of the past four months, as I learned key lessons about myself.

With adorable Christmas markets spreading across the piazzas of Florence in early December and only two weeks remaining before my flight home, I started to dread my departure.

"I can't imagine going back to normal life! What does it even feel like to stay in one place for more than a week?" I ranted to my roommate Shreya as we wandered through a holiday market.

"I know, it's going to be so weird to return to my childhood bedroom after living alone on a different continent for these past few months," Shreya lamented.

"Let's plan a final dinner all together with our Florence study-abroad *famiglia*. Gotta go out with a bang!" I proposed.

Shreya turned toward me and we had the same knowing look in our eyes. "Osteria Santo Spirito!" we both exclaimed in unison.

For the last dinner with my Florence famiglia, before we parted ways, we gathered at the same spot as our first dinner of the semester: an unassuming restaurant tucked into the corner of a piazza decently far from the city center, away from the crowds of tourists. This was the home of what we proclaimed the best meal in all of Italy—the three-cheese truffle gnocchi. The perfectly round pillows of soft gnocchi drowned in a creamy cheese sauce, dominated by the unmistakable aroma of truffle oil, often floats through my dreams, even to this day.

The 10 friends who had become my famiglia during our time in Florence were individuals I might never have met if I had simply stayed home and not ventured abroad. Fate brought us all together to live in *Via Ricasoli 38*, and our strong bonds had been formed through many laughs, blunders, and lifelong memories all across Europe during the past semester.

My initial fears of entering my semester in Florence not knowing anyone were replaced with pure *amore* for my famiglia. These were the people who I knew would always share my yearning for authentic Italian pizza, pasta, and gelato once we returned to New York City. Our continued reunions at Italian restaurants for years to come would prove that the bonds of study-abroad friendships never break, no matter how much distance or time elapses.

Midway through dinner, as everyone shared their favorite memory from the past semester, three of us, including myself, were pulled away by an email notification: our university's international business exchange program informed us of our application results for spending the following fall semester abroad again.

I opened the email and rejoiced—I had been accepted to the National University of Singapore and was officially going abroad again in just six months! My fears of returning to normal life dissipated. I now found my light at the end of the tunnel as I anticipated the dreary winter months back in New York City.

This was the moment when my life became a series of places between places. There was always somewhere I was coming from, always somewhere I was going next, and no sense of permanence in the place that I currently was in. From Florence that fall, to Tel Aviv that winter, to Singapore the following fall and beyond, I was always looking forward to the next big trip. In between trips, I was motivated to work harder now so I could play harder later.

My nomadic college journey awakened me to the concept that everything is just a transitory state. College, itself, is a place between places—between high school and adult life. I learned to embrace that transitory mindset, whether in physical transition between locations or in mental transition between states of mind.

Finding ways to thrive in change, rather than be thwarted by it, was a key part of growing into an adaptable individual who always relishes being in a place between places.

Europe: Lessons from Living in a Place between Places

*"If we were meant to stay in one place,
we'd have roots instead of feet."*

—Rachel Wolchin

Getting a taste of as many countries as possible became my overall travel philosophy.

Some people think that you can't possibly see a country and all it has to offer if you're only visiting for a weekend, or even just a day. These people are not wrong; you certainly cannot see everything in a short amount of time. But truly, how could you ever see *everything* a country and its diverse people have to offer?

In between nothing and everything lies *something*. Even just one day of experiencing a new country's scenery, culture, food, and language gives someone an exponentially deeper understanding of that country than someone who has never stepped foot within that country's borders. It's hard to quantify exactly how much more meaningful it is to spend three months in a place compared to three days.

I say, shoot for exponential growth in as many different locations and areas of understanding as possible, rather than focusing on exploring every last corner of one single country. As a kid, whenever my perfectionist tendencies stressed me out at school, my dad used to say: "Don't let perfection get in the way of good enough." The same applies to travel.

We learn the most when we know the least. Any traveler likely starts at zero: no knowledge of the architecture of a country's capital city, the types of food found on street corners, or what the language even looks when written or sounds like when spoken. To go from zero knowledge to any knowledge is still entirely impressive and worthwhile.

The idea that you must see "everything" in a place in order to make a trip there worthwhile is to endorse the notion that a sample spoonful of ice cream is not worth tasting. Enjoying life in small, limited doses is far better than only permitting yourself to enjoy things at the exact times when they can be experienced to their fullest. This is especially true because no one knows how long we will have to get around to whatever we are reserving for the perfect time and the fullest experience.

I fundamentally disagree with the "all or nothing" mentality that a lot of people have towards travel. I would rather take an overnight bus to Switzerland; walk across the covered bridges of Lucerne while admiring Mount Pilatus on a snowy day; pay $7 USD for the smallest possible Starbucks drink (painful to my wallet, but enlightening to my understanding of differences in costs of living around the world); eat cheese fondue properly for the first time in my life; learn about the rituals of *Carnival* celebrations; and then catch a bus back home to Florence in the span of 24 hours than never experience Switzerland at all.

This single day trip of less than 24 hours sparked a friendship with a Swiss exchange student named Ben during orientation week of my semester in Singapore.

In standard first-week-of-school, *let's-be-outgoing-and-make-friends* fashion, I hit him with the standard, "So where are you from?"

"Switzerland," Ben smiled.

"Oh my gosh, where? I was there last year, in Lucerne," I excitedly replied.

"You're kidding! That's my hometown."

That moment is the perfect embodiment of my ultimate goal in life: to be able to understand and relate to people, no matter where in the world they come from. To meet someone from a new country is exciting in its own right, but to then be able to add in your own excitement that you have been to their homeland, or even their exact hometown, means that you can, at some basic level, relate to them right off the bat. Knowing even just a taste of someone's culture opens up new doors for continued conversation, using your tidbits of information to wedge open the door even further to acquire a local perspective and a new friend.

Embracing a life of travel, no matter how long or short each trip may be, opens up opportunities for friendships and life lessons that simply would not exist without exposing yourself to as many places and perspectives as possible.

After spending every weekend in a different country for five months while studying abroad in Europe, constantly being in a place between places sparked a few key realizations that have shaped how I view travel.

Iceland

All throughout high school, my three best friends and I had joked, "I'm moving to Iceland," whenever life got rough. Right before I headed to Italy to spend four full months away from my best friends for the first time in years, we made our high school joke a reality, spending five blissful days soaking in the icy blue hot waters of the Blue Lagoon; snorkeling in between the continental plates in frigid sub-Arctic waters; exploring behind and underneath waterfalls; and spotting puffins on the grassy tops of black basalt cliffs. The rolling green hills felt straight out of a fantasy video game, while the crystals of broken icebergs that sparkled against the black sand of Diamond Beach put Tiffany jewelry stores to shame.

Ironically, what stands out most in my mind is not the otherworldly scenery, nor the kitschy local spots like the "best hot dog stand in Europe" made famous by a Bill Clinton visit. What I remember most is the whooping and jumping that ensued when my friends chased a giant bee out of our Airbnb; the laugh-until-you-cry hysteria of our Kylie Jenner-esque puffed lips after snorkeling in 2°C water; and our laughable blind faith in wandering around at 2 a.m. through the light-polluted city of Reykjavik where we most certainly wouldn't see the Northern Lights, but desperately tried to will them into existence with the pure power of imagination and desperation.

The most memorable moments that couldn't possibly be captured in a tourist booklet or a travel blogger's *Guide to Iceland* made this trip uniquely ours. I began to understand that travel derives its value and deep personal sentiment from these spontaneous, unpredictable, and sometimes mundane moments, not from a checklist of tourist attractions.

England

I approached the right side of the car, ready to get into the passenger seat, and was startled to see the steering wheel. *Duh*, I should've remembered that cars in the UK drive on the opposite side of the road. My friend Kieran and his dad sympathetically laughed at my simple foreigner mistake.

Kieran and I had never met in person before, but we had been Internet friends for years after meeting on Twitter. Finally getting the chance to visit him in his hometown of Norwich, England was a unique opportunity to see a less touristy part of a country through a local's perspective. As we walked around the streets of his hometown, Kieran pointed out notable shops and restaurants and his favorite pubs and gay bars. I learned to appreciate seeing a city through a local's eyes and am forever grateful to have experienced a part of England that most tourists don't see when they simply visit London and other major cities.

Cinque Terre, Italy

Cerulean waves crashed against the rocky cliffs as the pastel-colored houses of Cinque Terre looked down upon the Mediterranean Sea like seagulls perched along the coast. I mourned the loss of the new sneakers I mistakenly abandoned on the rocky beach and blamed my forgetfulness on the "drunk buckets"—a tourist specialty of the town of Monterosso. These beach buckets were filled to the brim with Italian *granitas* made with freshly cut fruit that completely masked the alcohol lurking in the mix. Moving on from trying to calculate the cost of my lost shoes, I quickly realized that the sneakers could be replaced. The priceless memories of my friends frolicking through the salty waves and laughing while drinking out of a giant bucket could not.

Amalfi Coast, Italy

If I heard a tour guide in a neon orange shirt and hat exclaim, "Follow the orange lady!" one more time, I was liable to spontaneously combust. Trading the personal chore of planning trip logistics for an all-inclusive group tour made just for study-abroad students seemed like a great idea until my friends and I realized that we had also traded away our freedom and autonomy. Missing the only time slot to see Capri's legendary Blue Grotto, dictated by the rising and falling tides, was beyond our control and simply at the fault of this "orange lady" who was our tour guide.

Our sketchy hostel was, again, booked by "the orange lady" and out of our control. These oceanside "bungalows" were crawling with bugs and lacked fans or air conditioning to give us a reprieve from the humid seaside air. My study-abroad buddies and I sat around a sad outdoor table under an umbrella on a rainy night, the unfortunate weather also being out of our control.

But making the most of an undesirable situation by laughing it all off, sipping €1 Peroni beers, and playing many rounds of get-to-know-you games late into the night *was* in our control, and ended up being the start of a beautiful friendship with my Florence *famiglia.* I learned to persevere and embrace the perspective that if you've already experienced the worst, everything can only go up from there.

Croatia

After disembarking from an overnight bus, crossing the border between Croatia and Slovenia on foot, and then getting a stamp in my passport for one of the only times during my semester in Europe, I thought a lot about what it meant to cross a border. How strange it was to realize that Europe was such an eclectic microcosm of nearly

50 incredibly diverse countries squeezed into a landmass about the same size as my home country, America. Since Croatia wasn't part of the Schengen Area, the "borderless" zone of 26 countries within Europe where most tourists can move around passport-free and visa-free, this was the first time during my first month abroad that I actually received a stamp in my passport.

The border patrol officer scrunched his eyes as he scrutinized my passport photo, then quickly looked up, smiled, and waved me through. Grabbing my passport back from him, I flipped through the remaining empty pages and made a silent promise to myself that these pages would be filled with colorful stamps from countries around the world over the next few years.

Germany

Taking an overnight bus once is enough of an ordeal—the chill of the incessant air conditioning making you deeply regret forgetting a blanket, the struggle to find a comfortable position for your arm and head against the window, and the occasional crying baby with no airplane engine to drown out the sound. Somehow, my friends and I thought that the overnight bus experience wasn't bad enough just once, but that it was essential to experience *two* nights in a row as we made our way from Florence to Munich for Oktoberfest, and then straight on from Munich to Berlin for the remainder of our long weekend.

Sleeping on a bus for two nights in a row meant that we didn't have to pay for a hostel or Airbnb! It seemed like a dream come true for college students on a tight budget, until we realized how two nights of low-quality sleep would leave us running on empty, with overworked immune systems as we walked through the rainy streets of Berlin.

Half of my friends stayed back dealing with cold symptoms, while three of us rallied to try to experience the infamous Berlin night-life, only to be told by a bouncer that showing up at midnight was "too early." Naively thinking that New York City was the only city that never sleeps, we learned to do our research by talking to lo-cals the next time we wanted to properly experience nightlife in a new country, and swore never to take back-to-back overnight buses ever again.

Slovenia

"Oh no, it's just me. Table for one."

The words felt foreign as they left my mouth. In *Gostilna Sokol*, a restaurant known for authentic Slovenian cuisine in Ljubljana's city center, I confronted the burning awkwardness of eating alone, a sometimes unavoidable part of solo travel, for the first time.

The hostess's lips pouted a bit as she put away the second menu she had picked up. *Goddamnit, stop pitying me!* I thought. Why did everyone have to assume I was sad and lonely because I was traveling alone? I made the conscious choice to go on this trip, and just because no one was available to go with me didn't mean I don't have any friends. Their schedules and travel priorities hadn't aligned with mine on this particular occasion.

My eyes followed the hostess's blonde head as she weaved past groups of cheerful locals and tourists, chattering and admiring the traditional paintings that lined the walls of this old town-house-turned-restaurant. I sat down at my table for one and beamed at the hostess with a smile much wider than necessary, as if to scream *I swear, I'm perfectly happy eating alone!*

I proudly ordered exactly what I wanted, knowing that I had cho-sen exactly where I wanted to eat at exactly the time I wanted to eat without having to compromise with any travel companions' conflicting desires. This first time eating alone taught me to embrace the opportunity to do exactly what I wanted without feeling held back by anyone else's preferences.

Poland

The blonde-haired, pale man chuckled as his blue eyes scanned me up and down while walking backwards and leading our tour group through his hometown of Krakow.

"You are joking, aren't you?" he responded, when I happily mentioned that I was half Polish. My dark brown hair, naturally tanned skin, and dark eyes were a stark contrast to the locals bustling through the streets around us.

"Nope! My dad's family is entirely Polish and I've grown up eating pierogies for dinner, enjoying *Kruschiki* at Christmas time, and singing *Sto lat* at every birthday," I happily chimed back. This was my first time visiting my fatherland, and traveling with friends meant I didn't have my dad there to visually back me up and prove my claim of ethnicity. The tour guide's reaction was an enlightening reminder that the United States' prevalence of multiethnic families and overall racial diversity was quite the opposite of a homogenous country like Poland.

Malta

Alone, again. Just because everyone else wanted to spend the weekend studying for midterms didn't mean I couldn't fulfill my dream of studying on the beaches of the tiny Mediterranean isle gems of Malta, Gozo, and Comino. This time, I confidently strode into a restaurant alone, asked for my table for one, and ordered a Maltese special: *stuffat tal-fenek*, or rabbit stew. I embraced the chance to sit at a table accompanied only by my thoughts. The next day, I walked the entire perimeter of the island of Comino by myself as the blue waves seemed to glow with a vibrant turquoise sparkle as they crashed against the limestone cliffs. I savored a moment that no one else but me would ever be able to play back in their mind. This memory was mine, and mine alone.

Spain

I woke up in the Barcelona airport, the sound of a janitor arousing me from my light slumber.

Oops. I wasn't supposed to be here. Flattening my body against the rows of hard plastic seats where passengers normally wait to board their flights, I barely took a breath as I tried to avoid being detected or questioned. My Spanish skills from high school were not reliable enough to function properly at 4 a.m., after having slept on a cold hard chair, with my small travel backpack as a pillow.

Why didn't I just stay at an Airbnb or hostel for that one night? It wasn't even a matter of money. It was my own fear of walking around Barcelona or being in a taxi alone after midnight as a girl who could only confidently bumble her way through *"Donde esta el baño?"*.

Luckily, the janitor didn't question me even though the airport supposedly had a policy of no overnight stays. I sighed and promised myself to actually brush up on the local language next time I was traveling alone. More importantly, I noted to not book flights that touched down in a new city after midnight, to avoid this situation in the future.

France

I crossed over the border from Spain to Ax-les-Thermes in the Pyrenees region of southwestern France with one goal only: to find the perfect crepe. I wandered through the quaint narrow streets that wove through pastel-colored houses until I reached the town square. There, the focal point was a small marble-lined pool where many visitors sat soaking their tired feet in the toasty waters fueled by the region's natural hot springs.

Around the corner, a yellow building with blue doors and bold blue lettering screaming *CREPERIE* invited me inside, where I was escorted to a garden lined with so much greenery I could have mistaken it for a portal to a jungle. The house specialty—a salted butter caramel crepe that oozed sugary sweetness punctured with notes of tangy salt—made the entire trip to this small French border town entirely worth it. Experiencing authentically-made food in its original birthplace was always worth the trip.

Denmark

On the first Friday of each November, Danes celebrate J-Day: the release of *Julebryg*, the annual Christmas beer. I was with my friend Nadja, who had once stayed with my family in my hometown while attending a few classes as an exchange student at my high school a few years prior. She excitedly led me down the cobblestone streets of her hometown, Odense, shortly before midnight.

When the clock struck midnight, the lights dimmed, Christmas lights twinkling rainbow colors pierced through the darkness, and waitresses with trays packed to the edges with bottles of Julebryg streamed out of the kitchen wearing Santa hats.

We clinked our bottles and cheered each other by exclaiming, *"Skål!"* to welcome the Christmas season, with my smile stretching from ear to ear. Pure joy radiated from every Dane in the room. Although my trip's timing had been a pure coincidence, I knew from then on that I should strive to align future trips with local holidays in different countries to get a true taste of each place's unique culture and celebrations.

Belgium

With my friend Wessel from the neighboring Netherlands as my somewhat local guide, we meandered through the dark streets of Brussels after checking out the infamous Delirium Café bar that boasts a menu of more than 2,000 beers from over 60 countries. With the unique taste of banana beer on our tongues, we reflected on our previous day in Bruges and how much nicer we'd found its clean streets and fairy tale-esque architecture and canals. Brussels seemed entirely lackluster in comparison. Had we not done our research, we may have only visited the capital, rather than exploring the surrounding, lesser-known cities.

We swore off ever coming back to Brussels and, instead, thanked ourselves for exploring the more quaint side of Belgium. After having experienced Wessel's Dutch hometown of Breda in comparison to Amsterdam, I had discovered firsthand that, much like visiting Kieran's hometown far outside of London, there was a certain charm and deeper understanding of what life is actually like for a local outside of a country's largest city. I thanked my early teenage self, who somehow had the foresight to make Internet friends on other continents, for these unique, authentic views of life in other countries.

Czech Republic

The castle-like structures of Prague's Old Town Square towered above the glittering village of small Christmas Market vendors in garland-lined huts. Locals and tourists alike strolled around carrying Santa-shaped mugs of hot mulled wine to ward off the chill of the December wind. I followed my friend Amy as she pointed out the surrounding restaurants and tiny local shops she had grown familiar with over the course of her semester in Prague. Much like how Florence had become my second home, Prague had become hers. Though she was Chinese-American rather than Czech, I was happy to get a tour of the city from a "local" who had earned that local status after five months of residing in the city of a hundred spires.

Our home university back in New York City was certainly not the only place where we could get a stellar education. In fact, our study abroad campuses at NYU Florence and NYU Prague weren't the prime locations for learning, either. The world around us, as it unfolded and revealed itself to us through each weekend's exploration of a new country, was a greater teacher than any professor or any textbook. I learned more from my life of constant movement than I ever could have learned from staying in one place.

Vietnam: A Crash Course in Empathy

"Travel is the only way to get empathy for other people's mindsets—to know their struggles and what they're drawn to."

—Abigail Spencer

I've always sworn to never get a tattoo that reminds me of someone because I don't want any physical markers on my body that might induce painful memories. However, that was before I met my dear friend, the Vietnamese motorbike.

I was dressed head to toe in a banana-print hat, banana-print button-down T-shirt, and banana-print baggy shorts. In any other country, my outfit would have constantly turned heads.

But in Cat Ba, Vietnam, the locals hardly took notice. My fellow tourists chuckled knowingly whenever my bright yellow ensemble came into view.

We'd just come from Hanoi, the nearby city where practically every souvenir salesman hawks apparel in these signature fruit-adorned patterns. The extremely crowded Sword Lake area of the city featured energetic street dancers, Jenga-stacking masters who needed to sit on someone's shoulders to reach the top of their towers, an array of backpackers touting photos to fund their further travels, and street market stalls that sold everything from sugar cane juice to fake Yeezys to banana-print outfits. I was one of over a dozen tourists I saw that night who became a proud owner of a full banana-print outfit.

We were all in on the inside joke that these outfits are nothing but absolutely iconic in Vietnam. If you don't believe me, a simple Google search for "Vietnam banana shirt" will show you how ubiquitous these truly are.

I was traveling in Vietnam with my friend Tony, who was also an exchange student at the National University of Singapore at the time. We had both been eager to see as much of Vietnam as we could in our long-but-short five-day weekend, which is how we found ourselves on Cat Ba Island in the middle of the beautiful Hạ Long Bay less than 24 hours after getting off our flight in Hanoi. Dressed head to toe in banana-print clothing, Tony and I were ready to maximize our time and cover as much ground as possible, which led us to renting a motorbike.

With my mother's warnings echoing in my head, the thought of riding a motorbike for the first time ever—in a foreign country, with no official knowledge of road rules—brought nothing but worry to my mind. But, the price of merely $8 USD for 24 hours of transportation made a motorbike rental impossible to refuse. Maybe I could silence that sound bite of my mom saying, "Make safe, smart decisions!" for just one day, for the sake of my college-student budget.

Biting my lip and trying to stifle my nerves, I sat my banana-print pants down on top of the hot leather seat that had been baking in the sun all morning. The humid air of a Vietnamese October day hugged my skin as I slid a helmet over my forehead, already full of perspiration.

I immediately felt out of my comfort zone as I placed my hands on the handlebars and tried to ignore the glaring impression that I was making a mistake, knowing how accident prone I am.

Before I could start overthinking the situation, a small Vietnamese woman approached me and made hand motions, telling me to get away from the motorbike. At first, I was perplexed why she was holding a large Aquafina water bottle full of yellow liquid, but as I stepped away, I realized this mysterious liquid was gas. I don't remember if I scoffed or rolled my eyes, but I should have. Finding out that the motorbike ran on low quality gas poured out of a water bottle that this woman picked up on the side of the road just moments earlier should have been a major red flag.

As the kind but non-English-speaking woman took a minute to fill up the tank, I stepped to the side and snapped a photo of myself in the bulky helmet, sweat dripping down my face as my tense brow and clenched jaw gave away my heightened level of nerves. In what would become an ironic (and iconic?) selfie, I took a Snapchat of myself wearing my helmet and my banana-print top, captioned it: "about to ride a motorbike, going to die," and sent it to my friends. Little did I know this would be my last non-emergency form of communication to friends and family that day.

The first hour on that motorbike passed by in the blink of an eye as I zoomed away from the bright-colored roofs and rickety buildings of Cat Ba, whose hodgepodge of similar yet divergent structures reminded me of the LEGO houses I built as a child. I cruised into a valley where lush green hills reminded me of dense fairytale forests where the trees held centuries of secrets. Triangular, conical peaks towered above me on either side.

Tony and I rode our bikes for almost an hour, hardly encountering any traffic at all. I relished the freedom of the wide-open road here in rural Vietnam. Just yesterday in Hanoi, the lack of clear crosswalks forced us to slowly walk across the road and simply hope for the best as motorbikes weaved their way around us. The ease of blitzing down an empty rural highway was a stark contrast to the anxiety-inducing, always-on state of high alert that was necessary for city driving.

As I revved the engine and my adrenaline spiked with every mile of asphalt that passed beneath the tires, I could not stop a grin from stretching ear to ear. The sound of the wind whistling past my ears mixing with the whirr of the motor created a white noise that allowed me to zone out and find a peace as pure as the verdant green Vietnamese countryside whizzing by in a blur.

I was queen of the road! And the motorbike was my trusty steed; a match made in heaven... until it wasn't.

One minute, I was flying down the traffic-free scenic road with no one in sight except for Tony on his motorbike right in front of me. The next minute, Tony's bike tipped over as it hit a pothole in the middle of the road. I panicked as my mind raced to process that Tony was lying on the road directly in front of me.

In that split second, the carefree bliss that I felt from zooming down the road with the wind in my face was replaced with a life-or-death decision. The life in question was Tony's, as I had been driving directly behind his motorbike and now—unless I changed course and swerved—I was about to run him over squarely in the middle of his legs and torso.

The mental image of my motorbike's wheels grinding over Tony's stomach at 60 kilometers per hour as he was sprawled out in the middle of the road ahead of me forced my disaster-aversion instinct to pull the handlebars swiftly to the right, veering off the road.

Time somehow simultaneously slowed down and went by in the blink of an eye as a kaleidoscope of colors flashed before my eyes: the black of the pavement, the gray of the gravel on the side of the road, the yellow of my banana-print clothing, the lime green of the motorbike's shiny exterior, and then the dark red of the blood flowing out of my knee, hands, and shin.

As I lay with my back on the ground, I tried to push the lime green bulky frame off of me, but the weight was too much. Tony ran over, somehow unscathed after toppling off of his own motorbike, and lifted the hefty frame off of me.

Without the bike's massive silhouette blocking my legs, my eyes flickered to the blood-soaked battlefield of my legs. In any other situation, my left leg alone would have caused me to burst into tears due to the various gaping red scrapes and cuts that made it look like someone had splatter painted it with red paint. But then I took in the full view of my right knee and started howling in both shock and pain as my brain registered that this was the deepest cut I'd ever experienced in my life. An entire flap of skin on the bottom half of my knee was open, bleeding, and showing white on the interior.

My mother's warning about making safe, smart decisions reverberated in my mind. The guilt of disobeying her only made me cry even more. There was no easy way I could tell her about this accident. I had made a bad decision and was facing the consequences.

I can only imagine the confusion going through the mind of the European backpacker who happened to be driving by at that moment: trying to make sense of two toppled motorbikes, two banana-suited individuals, and my incessant crying and screaming. He pulled his own motorbike to the side of the road and quickly jogged over to Tony and me.

This entire interaction was a blur as my fight or flight instincts had kicked in and dedicated all of my brain's available attention to the gaping hole in my knee. However, the one snippet I do remember was this man calmly saying, "You'll be just fine, all you need are some stitches."

My mind did a double take as I snapped back, "Stitches! What do you mean stitches!?"

My heart rate increased exponentially as I tried to rack my brain for anything I knew about stitches—nothing. I had never before broken a bone in my body, undergone any serious medical procedure, or even dealt with pain remotely close to this. My worst physical mishap in the past was somehow spraining my pinky finger by smacking my hand into my dad's at a bad angle while giving him a high five. This injury was now on a whole different level, and worries about the worst-case scenario ricocheted around my brain as my brow furrowed and my heart rate quickened.

I was about to dive headfirst into an unfamiliar procedure, in an unfamiliar country. The kind European backpacker kept talking to Tony and me, while trying to bandage my knee with some scraps of linen, to at least temporarily stop the bleeding. We collectively came to the realization that we were in the middle of rural Vietnam with no cell signal and not even the faintest idea if a hospital even existed nearby, let alone how we would be able to get there, given our lack of transportation and my inability to walk.

Thankfully, my cries and screams had attracted attention from some locals who lived down the road, so a crowd of onlookers had started to form. Though it was clear no one in this rural area of Vietnam spoke English, one man must have recognized the word "hospital" in our frantic discussion and managed to communicate through hand signals that I could get on the back of his motorbike and he would drive me to the nearest hospital, just a few miles away.

It was at this point that I said goodbye to my now-frenemy, the Vietnamese motorbike, with its lime green exterior glowing in the golden hour lighting as the sun set on our time together. I was too preoccupied with my own injuries to realize that the bike had sustained its own damage. Flecks of glass from the rearview mirrors that had broken off upon contact with the pavement sparkled in the early evening light as I drove off in the opposite direction, clinging tightly to a total stranger, holding my leg straight out on the side of the motorbike in an effort not to bend my knee and cause the wound to open even more.

This sweet man from the local village took me directly to a nearby hospital that was nestled in the hills of Cat Ba, so hidden behind the lush scenery that I never would have found it myself if I had been walking along the main road. As the odd sight of a banana-print-adorned girl whose arms were wrapped around a middle-aged Vietnamese man rolled into view of the hospital windows, I expected someone to come running out. However, the area seemed nearly deserted, with barely any signs of life— no jackets on the backs of chairs, no pens on the desktops. I was starting to wonder if the hospital was even open or properly staffed when Tony rolled up on his own motorbike and the kind stranger who had let me cling onto him for dear life made his way back to his home.

Each time I took a step and placed pressure on my right leg, the one with the deep knee wound, a lightning bolt of pain electrified my body. It took great effort to keep my leg as straight as possible without bending my knee and opening the wound. I shifted my weight from side to side, like a pirate with a peg leg.

We made our way inside the hospital and quickly realized that the doctors there spoke absolutely no English. I started to panic, but realized that blood and open wounds are, thankfully, a universal language. My frantic pointing at my bleeding legs, coupled with the look of sheer fear and pain on my face, must have gotten the point across because the two doctors whisked me off to a hospital room where they could lie me down and take a close look.

The doctors didn't need much translation to come to the same conclusion the European backpacker had primed me for: I needed stitches. Since I couldn't be briefed about what the doctors had in mind for mending my knee, I resigned myself to blind faith as I laid on a table in this makeshift ER in rural Vietnam, getting anesthesia injections and stitches in my leg.

Somehow, the local anesthesia shot in my leg felt like it didn't work because I felt every single motion of the needle as it passed through my skin and began to close up the wound. Because I didn't know how to emotionally deal with what was going on, I found myself hysterically laughing. I had no idea why this was my first reaction to the pain, but being ever the optimist, I assume my brain thought it was somehow better to laugh and make a joke out of this than to cry.

After the doctors stepped away and signaled that they were done with the surgery, I looked down at the nine stitches in my leg and nearly burst into tears again at the sight of my poor knee looking like an ugly Frankenstein. Thoughts of never being able to wear a skirt or shorts again for fear of how ugly my knee would look immediately rushed to my mind. Somehow, society had ingrained in me that this was one of the first things I should be worried about after a knee surgery.

I gently swung my legs off the surgery bed, taking caution to keep both knees incredibly straight, and gingerly put my weight on my leg as I stood up. I managed to hobble to the next room, where

Tony was struggling to use Google Translate in offline mode to prompt the nurse to type out Vietnamese words and convert them into English. As we tried to decipher the dosage instructions written in Vietnamese on the bottle of painkillers, I had never been so thankful for the existence of Google Translate. Whoever initially invented the translation app probably never would have imagined this scenario as a prime use case.

Once technology (and the international health insurance provided by my study abroad program) had saved the day, I paid a mere $75 dollars for the whole procedure, collected my pain medication, and exited the hospital. Standing in front of that rural Vietnamese hospital, with my bloody knees stitched up beneath thick white bandages, wearing my ridiculous banana outfit... I smiled for a photo. I felt like I needed a picture to prove that it even happened, because the whole scenario was utterly ridiculous, unexpected, and unbelievable. As I clung to Tony on the back of his motorbike like a baby monkey clutching its mother's back, we slowly, carefully, made our way back to our hostel in Cat Ba.

For hours, I simply laid in bed alone thanks to my new inability to bend my knees. Even a trip down the hall to the bathroom brought tears to my eyes as each step applied pressure to the areas of my skin that were screaming out for reprieve after being slashed open and stitched back together just a few hours earlier.

Tony returned with fresh *banh mi* sandwiches from a cart in the street, one of the best and most authentic ways to get this treat in Vietnam. Soon after, I struggled through tears and discomfort as I attempted to fall asleep, settling into the reality that what had just happened, had actually just happened.

The next morning, channeling the energy of Broadway and the city of New York that I missed so dearly, I told myself the show must go on. I mustered all my strength to limp along and bear the pain of my throbbing injury to continue our trip, with three full days left to go.

I knew I wouldn't be able to navigate going to an airport, carrying my luggage, and traveling back from the Singapore airport to my apartment all by myself in my current physical state. And I also knew I didn't want to ruin Tony's trip by suggesting that he should sacrifice the rest of his time in Vietnam by accompanying me back to Singapore.

I found a way to make do with shuffling along and dragging my leg in a certain way that elicited the least pain and the least wincing. With great effort, I kept plugging along on our itinerary of touring Hạ Long Bay.

Later that night, after a four-hour ride back to Hanoi, my friend Chloe from NYU who is from Hanoi, arranged for her sister and family friend to take me to a hospital to get my wounds and stitches checked and to translate since the doctors only spoke Vietnamese. The two were incredibly sympathetic and helpful, even buying me food and drinks and snacks before dropping me off at the airport after the doctor checkup. It still amazes me that I'm lucky enough to have friends in all different parts of the world who will go out of their way to help me, and I'm incredibly grateful for that.

Empathy and the desire to help others are innate for all of us and should be a fundamental part of the human experience, no matter where you are in the world. The next day, I was alone for about an hour while Tony finished up exploring Hanoi on his own before meeting me at the airport. I ended up breaking down crying in the airport lobby when I just couldn't muster the strength to keep pushing a cart with my heavy travel backpack. A few Vietnamese strangers came up to me since they noticed I was crying, and although I couldn't explain anything and they couldn't properly offer help due to the language barrier, it reminded me how human emotions permeate cultural divides, without needing translation.

Even on my flight to our next destination, Ho Chi Minh, the flight attendants were incredibly sympathetic to the girl with two huge wounds on her knees. I was able to evoke enough pity to get myself an entire row to myself to stretch out my legs in their unbendable state.

Once settled into our hostel in Ho Chi Minh, I sadly canceled my day trip to the Mui Ne desert the next day as I needed to see a doctor every 24 hours to check if my wound had become infected. I couldn't possibly take a full day trip to the desert to ride ATVs across the sand dunes at sunset. Instead, I took it slow, limping around the city by myself at the pace of a turtle.

Staying behind allowed me time to confront my own ignorance about the Vietnam War. I decided to go to the War Remnants Museum. Wandering around by myself, I spent a few hours diving into the Vietnam War—or "American War" from the Vietnamese perspective—at the War Remnants Museum.

When I learned about the Vietnam War in high school, I never fully grasped the gravity of the conflict and how the entire world essentially was calling for the US to evacuate Vietnam. It saddened me to read the museum exhibits explaining how the US government fundamentally misunderstood who their enemy even was. An entire section of the museum showcasing photographs of the after-effects of Agent Orange struck me. Tears filled my eyes from seeing people who became disabled due to the actions of the US, and in a way that could have been completely avoided.

Limping around the Vietnam War Museum, while reading about disabled individuals, gave me a rather strong sense of irony and a deeper sense of empathy for those with disabilities inflicted upon them. The past few days with my leg, I had also observed that people treated me or reacted to me quite differently whether my injury, or temporary disability, was visible or not.

When I wore long pants and no one could see the bandages on my knees, I got many dirty looks for limping/ walking so slow and holding up the line to disembark a bus or ascend a staircase. However, when I wore shorts and the huge bandages on my knees made it visibly obvious that I was injured, I got much more sympathetic looks, and many people even stopped to inquire what had happened to me. I now look back on this experience as a lesson in empathy; not all injuries or disabilities are visible and we shouldn't be so quick to judge others who might be dealing with unseen physical or mental issues.

The next day after visiting the War Museum, I was on a guided tour of the Cu Chi tunnels, which were built and used by the Viet Cong during the war to outsmart the American troops. Our tour guide, who called himself Mr. Bean instead of his true name, Mr. Binh, was a Vietnamese man who fought in the war as an intelligence agent for the Americans, so he was perfectly poised to reveal both the American and Vietnamese perspectives of the war.

Mr. Binh wisely proclaimed, "You can't truly understand the war and what it was like if you've never shot a gun before, so I encourage you to take this opportunity to shoot an actual AK-47 on the shooting range here at the tunnels!"

That point about truly understanding the war and putting myself in the shoes of the soldiers made sense to me, so I donned protective earmuffs and stepped up to the massive gun. Having never shot even a small handgun before, I picked up the AK-47 and aimed at the fake targets across the field. After only firing five shots, I gained great sympathy for the soldiers dealing with that sound, that shock of the bullet zipping forward, and the recoil of the gun on a daily, or hourly, basis during war.

With these new perspectives on war swimming in my mind, I processed the irony of joking with friends that I had gotten a "battle scar" from Vietnam from my motorbike accident. Years later, as I thought about this near-death experience in the context of a country once ravaged and shaped by war, I jotted down an open letter to the motorbike in the Notes app on my phone:

"Dear Vietnamese motorbike, thank you. Had I never decided to take a chance on you and ride a motorbike for the first time that fateful day, my life would be quite different. You helped me discover firsthand that when traveling and putting myself in unfamiliar situations, life finds a way to teach me the hardest lessons that I didn't even know I needed.

Now, every day I wake up with a scar on my right knee. It's nowhere near as gruesome as it initially looked—time can heal most anything—but this scar has now become a part of me that will always be a constant reminder of you and that day in Vietnam. It's not only a reminder of that time I took a risk, but also how I experienced the euphoria of pure, blissful freedom riding down the open road surrounded by the breathtaking hills of Cat Ba, enjoying that one moment to its fullest.

It's a reminder of the Vietnam War victims and survivors, who dealt with their own mental and physical scars much more serious than my own. It's a reminder of those lessons in empathy, and a call to action to offer help and forgiveness whether or not someone appears to have an injury or disability. Now I know that there's always a deeper story to someone's struggle, and every scar tells a story."

It's not quite a tattoo, but that scar on my right knee is just as permanent, and just as painful a reminder, of the mix of heart-wrenching moments, but also the enlightening insights, that I experienced in Vietnam.

Japan and Laos:
Expectations vs. Reality

*"The traveler sees what he sees,
the tourist sees what he has come to see."*

—Gilbert K. Chesterton

As the plane descended over the twinkling lights of Tokyo, my headphones blared The Strokes's "Welcome to Japan," Halsey's "Tokyo Narita," and Shawn Mendes's "Lost in Japan" in rapid succession. I had been hyping myself up to visit Japan for years, while listening to these songs in my hometown bedroom, and now I was finally lucky enough to step into the real-life version of this country described so fondly in song.

For most of my life, whenever the word "Japan" escaped from someone's lips it was accompanied by a glimmer in their eyes. Perhaps it was the country's aura of advancement, culture of efficiency, and affinity for new technologies that made it seem like such a high-tech utopia. Or maybe the pervasive export of Japanese culture, from anime to Nintendo video games to J-Pop to Japanese cuisine, had always created a "cool" factor.

Japan's legacy of ancient history and traditional beauty coexists with extensive modernization. The land of the rising sun draws visitors to natural wonders like snow-capped Mount Fuji, as well as metropolitan wonders like Shibuya Crossing, the busiest pedestrian crossing in the largest city in the world where the energy of hundreds of people zig-zagging across the street hums louder than the busiest beehive.

After having heard friends, family, and seemingly everyone in pop culture rave about the wonders of Japan, I made a steadfast decision to visit Japan during the fall break of my semester abroad in Singapore. In my mind, Japan promised to be nothing short of incredible. Everything I had ever heard, read, or watched about the country, set my expectations exceedingly high.

However, my first night in Japan was nothing like I expected.

Rain splattered against the bus windows and the numbers on the dashboard's digital clock crept into the single digits of the early morning. My fellow travelers Jack and Alex, who were also exchange students in Singapore with me, followed me onto the last affordable airport shuttle. Our destination was a capsule hostel—a Japanese invention that solved city space constraints by placing beds in small pods separated by claustrophobia-inducing walls and a curtain at the entrance of the bed near your feet.

Traveling with a group can be challenging. It requires constant negotiation on timing, food, sleeping arrangements, itinerary, etc. This trip to Japan was no different. Jack's Irish accent, Alex's Canadian accent, and my own boisterous American accent stood out amidst the hushed tones of the Japanese travelers around us as we discussed the drama that transpired that night. Thanks to a few petty disagreements and severe miscommunication, my group of six exchange student travel buddies had dwindled down to three.

"It's not our fault they missed the last shuttle!" quipped Jack.

"Yeah, they're the ones who were being petty and not speaking to us," agreed Alex.

"I feel bad... but also I don't. They're the ones who intentionally locked us out of our Airbnb in Seoul yesterday. Karma is a bitch," I shrugged.

Somewhere ahead of us on the route from the airport to central Tokyo, the three other girls we had been traveling with were in an expensive Uber on their way to the same capsule hostel. Tense texts were exchanged and abrupt exits from group chats were made. They were furious that we had somehow caused them to miss the last shuttle. From our perspective, they were perfectly capable of finding it themselves and were unfairly placing blame on us.

When we arrived at the hostel, there was no receptionist in sight, understandable for the late-night check-in, but also perfectly reflective of Japan's culture of automation and increasing lack of human contact. In a country where many prefer to order food from vending machines and select sushi from conveyor belts rather than engaging with servers, a self check-in was nothing but par for the course.

Yet our first taste of automation and contactless service ended up somehow leaving us with only two sleeping pod reservations. Alex wasn't registered to stay at the hostel for that night. The next day, we realized that it was our own human error, not automation, to blame, since Alex mistakenly booked a hostel by the same name in a different neighborhood of Tokyo.

But at the time, we were nothing but frustrated, confused, and suddenly hungry. We left the hostel lobby and headed out to explore the rainy streets of Tokyo. Our mission: find a snack somewhere at nearly 4 a.m.

Shuffling through puddles that lined the streets of the Asakusa neighborhood of Tokyo, we wandered past the Senso-ji temple, traditional street-food stalls, and streets lined with casual *izakaya* bars. All were shrouded in darkness at this early morning hour, leaving it up to our imaginations to form a first impression of what these streets might actually look like during the day with tourists and locals exchanging money and smiles.

Even small, seemingly unimportant alleyways were home to various vending machines selling beverages and snacks on unassuming street corners.

"Wow, you don't even need to talk to a human at a convenience store here," I thought to myself. Back home, vending machines populated malls and college dorm buildings, not street corners. The Japanese value for efficiency and contactless transactions was apparent everywhere.

Seeking some form of human interaction, or maybe just the bright lights and wide selection of a real convenience store, we skirted around the vending machines and headed into a Family Mart.

Walking into this popular Japanese convenience store chain, I thought back to the first time I entered a Family Mart when I visited my friend Sahitya during her semester abroad in Shanghai. The "Family Mart smell" as she described it—a product of the mysterious meats on a stick that sat on the counter next to the cashier— now hit my nose here in Japan and jolted me awake.

Browsing the aisles of a grocery or convenience store in a new country is often one of the best ways to feel immediately immersed in a new environment. The various products and brands you see, which register as strikingly unfamiliar, are, in fact, so mundane and common that they are convenience-store items. This is a unique gauge of what products are part of everyday life in a new corner of the world.

We walked through aisles of little seaweed-wrapped triangles of rice called *onigiri*, individually-wrapped fluffy Asian breads, and the widest variety of Kit Kats I had ever seen. The American chocolate brand was an anomalous hit in Japan thanks to clever marketing: the Japanese phrase *kitto katsu*, meaning "you will surely win," helped the candy bars gain popularity among Japanese students who viewed them as tokens of good luck. Unique Japan-exclusive Kit Kat flavors ranged from *sake* to *wasabi* to strawberry cheesecake to grape. I intended to try them all before leaving Japan.

With our foreign convenience store experience serving as our informal introductory glimpse of Japanese culture, we left the Family Mart smell behind us and walked out into the fresh rain.

The glow of the street lights and neon signs reflected in the rainwater that pooled on the streets. As we splashed our tired feet across the slippery pavement, we came upon an unassuming round yellow reflection in the middle of one puddle: a lemon. This random fruit on the street was as out of place as we were—an American, an Irishman, and a Canadian getting lost in the streets of Tokyo in the middle of the night.

I suddenly became a spectator for an impromptu game of Tokyo street fruit soccer as Alex stepped over to the lemon and started kicking it back and forth with Jack.

"When life gives you lemons..." started Jack,

"...make lemonade," finished Alex, as he stomped on the poor, beat-up fruit and split it into two. Lemon juice sprayed out and mixed with the raindrops that already glistened on the pavement.

Laughing about our strange, late-night jaunt around Tokyo, we made our way back to the hostel, deciding how to sneak Alex inside for the night, even though he didn't seem to have a proper reservation.

That first rainy night, sadly, turned out to be a preview of the entire week. We were the unlucky victims of typhoon season in Japan, casting the city of Tokyo into a dreary, drizzly haze, at best, and a thundering downpour, at worst. My plan to trek up Mt. Fuji was washed away by the typhoon. Tired of trudging through the rain after a long first day of language barriers and prices that shocked our student budgets, our first dinner in Japan ended up being the first budget-friendly place we could find—Mexican food, despite being in the mecca of authentic Japanese sushi, ramen, *takoyaki*, and more.

Nothing I expected about Japan ended up going according to plan. Based on previous travelers' experiences, I expected to leave Japan in absolute wonder and awe. But mistakes piled up, the weather worsened, and every potential restaurant or activity turned out to be incredibly cruel to our dwindling student budgets. It seemed that every day whatever could possibly go wrong, did go wrong. My traveler's mindset of adaptability and flexibility got its greatest workout trying to make the most of unexpected situations and experiences that didn't fit the mold of my high expectations.

I didn't hate Japan—the trip was, overall, enjoyable, and I would still recommend anyone visit. However, the less-than-ideal weather and unexpected interpersonal dynamics made it hard to enjoy the country to its fullest potential. I regretted not being able to walk away from my Japan trip with the perfect experiences and memories that everyone else seemed to have when they spoke so highly of the country.

Visiting Japan was a lesson in not letting high expectations create a disappointing view of reality. I started to wonder what it might be like to visit a place with no expectations at all, and to see how that might affect my experience.

At the time, I had no idea that in just a few short weeks, Laos would teach me this contrasting lesson.

After 16 weeks living in Singapore, I had made full use of my 6-day weekends. This was possible by stacking my classes into a packed 12-hour back-to-back Thursday schedule. I had visited nearly all the countries in Southeast Asia, with immigration stamps from Indonesia, Vietnam, Thailand, the Philippines, Malaysia, Cambodia, and Myanmar already decorating the interior of my passport in an array of colors, languages, and visas of various shapes and sizes.

Throughout the semester, these were the countries that frequently rolled off the tongues of fellow exchange students seeking to visit the most iconic cities and tourist attractions. But one last country in Southeast Asia seemed to be largely neglected: Laos. Perhaps it was unpopular because no one knew how to properly pronounce it (is the *s* silent or not?) or because the visa was quite pricey. But, for whatever reason, no one I knew out of the nearly 2,000 exchange students in my program in Singapore had yet chosen to visit Laos that semester.

Not wanting to neglect any country in Southeast Asia, no matter how little I had previously heard about it, I set my sights on Laos as my last big trip before finals week. My go-to travel buddy Maddy was also eager to explore this relatively unknown territory, along with our equally curious fellow exchange student Shannon. To us three American college students, the fact that we knew almost nothing about the country and didn't have the slightest idea of what were the typical things for a tourist to see there made the trip all the more enticing.

From previous trips that semester, I had learned my lesson the hard way about hyping up a place too much, and arriving with unrealistic expectations based off of Instagram photos or travel blogs that made exaggerated claims about a country's pristine, shiny tourist attractions.

In Taiwan, I expected to taste the best bubble tea of my life in its place of origin, but ended up sorely disappointed. Somehow, I preferred the American version I had grown accustomed to at home.

In Myanmar, I expected to be dazzled by glimmering temples, but ended up agreeing with an article that deemed the capital, Yangon "just a dirty, boring city."

This time around for Laos, I decided to do the bare minimum to keep my expectations in check. I didn't look up endless archives of photos. I didn't scour the Internet for blog posts about what to see and do. I didn't even map out a full itinerary of places to visit. I packed my bags for Laos with no prior knowledge, and no expectations, for the first time.

The only thing I booked in advance was a guided tour on a slow-sailing wooden longboat that would meander down the mighty Mekong River for two days. This slow boat journey would transport Maddy, Shannon, and me from the riverside city of Luang Prabang, Laos to the border of Thailand. This unique mode of transportation was not only a way to revel in the beauty of the Mekong Delta, but also a way to connect with a local.

Suly, our local guide, is a woman who I will never forget. Over the course of our two-day journey down the river, she spent nearly every minute with Maddy, Shannon, and me as the lone passengers on our long wooden boat. We eagerly listened as Suly explained her entire life story, from growing up in a mountain village and surviving a near-death experience with a bicycle, to learning how to speak English and moving to the city of Luang Prabang, to establishing herself as a female entrepreneur who had dreams of writing a book about her life one day.

Never did I imagine that signing up for this slow boat tour would mean having the opportunity to meet a guide who ended up becoming a true friend who brings me joy and inspires me. To this day, whenever I see Suly's updates and photos on my Facebook feed, my heart smiles and I feel as if I am once again basking in the warmth of the Lao sun. Three years after we first met, I was even able to visit Suly in her new home on San Juan Island, off the coast of Seattle, after she had married an American man and started a new life in America with a child of her own.

In addition to kind locals-turned-friends like Suly, my trip to Laos featured some of the most unexpectedly good food I had tasted in the five months I spent living in Asia. A dish called *kaipaen*, also known as dried river weed, still lingers on my taste buds. I never knew it was a local specialty until we happened to sit down at a hole-in-the-wall restaurant to order it. We enjoyed our river weed with a cold Beerlao, a local rice brew that turned out to be arguably the best beer in Southeast Asia.

Unlike the images of fresh-from-the-ocean sushi, steaming hot and rich ramen, and authentic matcha that I expected before ever even stepping foot in Japan, the cuisine in Laos surpassed all of my expectations, precisely because I had no preconceived notions of Lao food to begin with.

Aside from distinctive meals bursting with regional ingredients that I still crave to this day, my time in Laos led me through explosive orange sunsets atop the sacred Mount Phou Si, the icy blue tranquility of Kuang Si Waterfall, and the muddy brown waters of the Mekong that lapped up against the trunks of wild elephants lining the riverbank to drink.

Each unexpected sight, taste, and feeling led me closer and closer to the notion that Laos was my favorite country in all of Asia—a hidden gem among the neighboring countries tourists tend to flock to.

After experiencing the serendipitous joy of my time in Laos, I resolved to maintain this mentality of focusing on reality, not expectations. I've learned to level my expectations in order to maximize potential enjoyment, rather than having unrealistic visions of perfection that real life could never manifest.

When people ask me where I see myself in five years, I love to answer with an honest, "I have no idea, and I don't intend on figuring it out." Travel has taught me that not having any preconceived notions nearly eliminates the ability to be disappointed. If you allow yourself to live in the moment, without absorbing opinions and expectations from the people and media surrounding you, life becomes more about the journey of discovery.

Laos always serves as a reminder that it is better to try doing something new out of pure curiosity than to set out with explicit expectations of grandeur. Instead, I've learned to show up, look around, and enter new experiences with an open mind. Sometimes, it's better to not know what you're getting yourself into and just let life unfold in its surprisingly beautiful way.

Malaysia: Awakening a Mixed-Race Perspective

*"Multi-culture is the real culture of the world—
the pure race doesn't exist."*
—Keanu Reeves

"I hope you two are enjoying your evening together! Ma'am, you look lovely. Would you two like to order any drinks?" asked the waiter, tossing in a wink.

I cringed inside as I tried to picture this scenario from the perspective of the waiter. On one side of the table was me: a young girl whose golden-brown skin hinted at Southeast Asian descent, dressed up for a nice evening out in Kuala Lumpur, Malaysia. On the other side of the table: a middle-aged, well-dressed white man who kept encouraging me to have a lavish evening. "Get whatever you want! It's my treat," he chimed in.

No, this man was not a sugar daddy or a Western traveler who had hired an escort during a visit to Malaysia, as the waiter seemed to assume, judging by his suggestive commentary and behavior. This was my dad.

I had been living in Singapore during a semester abroad as an exchange student, and my dad had scheduled a business trip to visit some coworkers in Singapore. Our schedules had miraculously aligned, so I immediately booked us a weekend trip to the capital of Malaysia. I thought visiting Kuala Lumpur would be a great opportunity to explore a new country with my dad before he returned home to the United States.

What I didn't think about was the fact that this was the first time I had ever taken a trip with just my dad. A daddy-daughter trip seemed so innocent and wholesome in my eyes, and the thought of how other people might perceive the two of us together didn't even cross my father's mind. But I quickly realized that we were drawing stares and whispers from the onlookers around us. In Kuala Lumpur, a hotspot for sex tourism among wealthy Westerners, the sight of a white man with a young Southeast Asian girl did *not* cause most people to think, "Ah, look at that man and his daughter."

As the waiter lit up a candle and seemed intent on setting a mood, I tried to quickly clear the confusion. Making sure the waiter was listening, I loudly prompted, "Hey *Dad*, what would you like to order?"

Ever so subtly, the waiter's face flashed with a look of confusion as his brow furrowed slightly. Then, a wave of understanding rippled across his face as his facial muscles untensed and his cheeks flushed, perhaps showing his embarrassment.

He understood that he was no longer in charge of setting the mood for a romantic rendezvous; he was serving a father and a daughter, who just happen to look nothing alike. If only my mother, who is Filipino, and who shares more physical features with me, had been there to make the puzzle pieces click into place, bridging the gap between me and my white father, who is of Polish descent.

The rest of the evening, I tried to just enjoy the Malaysian local delicacies of *mee goreng* (spicy fried noodles) and *nasi lemak* (coconut milk rice and crispy anchovies), but my mind kept taking the perspective of a third party. I tried to imagine what other people thought when they passed by and observed me enjoying a dinner with my father.

I quickly recalled the past few days and grew internally morti-fied when I imagined what the hotel front desk clerk might have thought when my father and I casually strolled up and asked to check into our room.

Interracial race couples and mixed-race children have become more normalized in America over the past few years: the percent-age of Americans identifying with two or more races is project-ed to be the fastest-growing racial or ethnic group in the coming decades. It's certainly not as common in Asia and I was starting to understand firsthand how an outsider's perceptions of my dad and I could be easily misconstrued in a region where sex tourism comprised a significant portion of the underground economy.

Looking back, I try to laugh off this situation and tell it as a fun-ny anecdote about cultural differences and varying norms in dis-parate regions of the world. But in that moment, I had never felt such a loss of control of my own narrative. That night, I experi-enced the role that stereotypes play in our lives.

People mean well, but there is no easy way to turn off the human brain's desire to categorize everything in digestible, comprehensi-ble packages. I get excited every time I see a mixed-race or multi-racial family portrayed in film or on advertisements, because the more people around the world get exposed to this concept, the less confusing the mixed-race experience will be. Representation matters, and because most media shows family units with a con-sistent skin tone and similar features, most people do not assume a father-daughter relationship upon seeing a white man with a younger Asian girl.

When I was in elementary school, I had been happily attending soccer practice one afternoon while my dad cheered me on from the sidelines. During our half-time break, when my teammates and I eagerly ran off the field to stuff our faces with orange slices as energy boosters, I ran over to my dad and gave him a high five as he beamed from ear to ear. Orange slices with a side of positive affirmation from my dad made my eight-year-old self feel on top of the world.

But then, a young boy from my soccer team came over and interrupted my glee with an ignorant quip that will never erase itself from my memory: "Are you adopted? Why don't you look like your dad?"

To me, my parents were my parents. To suggest that I was anything out of the ordinary was to wedge a knife of doubt and uncertainty into my impressionable mind. Ten-year-old me was taken aback, embarrassed, offended, and completely dumbfounded by that question. I felt self-conscious every subsequent time my dad would come to a soccer game without my mom also accompanying him, since her tan skin and dark hair matching my own visually verified that I was in fact my mother's child.

I don't remember the exact moment I realized that it was uncommon for parents to not share an ethnic background, but I do remember the *after.* Once I understood that my parents were unique, I started noticing the discrepancies everywhere: how my friends' parents' skin tones matched one another, how other parents jointly favored the same cuisine from their motherland, and how my friends never had to learned how to sing "Happy Birthday" in two different mother tongues.

Almost all of my friends, neighbors, and classmates were white, so my childhood self thought that, surely, I must fall into that category. Why would I want to not belong in the majority? When standardized tests in elementary school asked me to fill in a bubble to indicate my ethnicity and I could only choose one, I selected "White" instead of "Asian," despite the fact that my eternally golden-brown skin starkly contrasted that of my white friends. Back then, there was no checkbox for "Mixed-race or multiracial," which is what I proudly check off today.

Growing up, my mom never taught me Tagalog, the native Filipino language, since she didn't want my dad to feel like she and I had a secret language he didn't understand. This lack of connection to the native language now makes it hard for me to relate to fully Filipino individuals who were raised in a household with two Filipino parents.

As a young adult, I joined the International Filipino Association club at my university and felt out of place even though I looked similar to the other Filipino international students and Filipino-American students around me. I didn't understand the jokes in Tagalog, I wasn't familiar with all types of Filipino cuisine, I didn't have yearly visits to family in the Philippines to reminisce about. I was Filipino, but not Filipino *enough.*

During my semesters abroad in Singapore and Europe, I had the chance to travel to both the Philippines and Poland by myself, to satiate my curiosity about the different motherlands of both my parents. Both places were able to evoke a feeling of home for me, even if I didn't quite fit in with the native inhabitants.

When I visited the Philippines, I didn't feel quite Filipino because I couldn't speak the language and I still had a Western look, with my height especially making me stand out in a place where most girls are short. Likewise, when I visited Poland and told my Airbnb host and local guides that I was half Polish, they looked at me in disbelief, as if expecting me to say, "Just kidding!" Again, I wasn't Polish *enough.*

Even though the locals might have given me the impression that I was an outsider in their homeland, I felt just as comforted by the familiarity of both cultures and foods in the Philippines and Poland. I'd grown up eating pierogies and kielbasa from Polish cuisine as well as *ensaymada* sweet cheese rolls, chicken adobo, and ube-based desserts from Filipino cuisine.

Much like these two food groups coexisting in my household kitchen, the two parts of my ethnicity and heritage can coexist within me. I've realized I don't have to be *enough* of anything.

Traveling to different environments challenged my conception of self and made me aware of how onlookers could be putting me into categories that I don't quite agree with. Through reflecting on these experiences, I gained the strength to know that identifying with parts of my ethnic background doesn't have to be justified or approved by anyone else; just being uniquely myself is enough. I hope that anyone who's struggling with a mixed identity can embrace the fact that being different is a strength, not a point of embarrassment. You don't have to be "enough" of any part of your various cultures. You are enough just the way you are.

Despite our best wishes, the world around us does tend to judge a book by its cover and make certain assumptions based on outward appearance. After realizing that I have no control over the stereotypes, narratives, and preconceived notions that people ascribe to me, I made a conscious decision to focus on the parts of me and my identity that I *can* control, rather than letting myself spiral into self-doubt and an internal identity crisis on the basis of perceived race. I could let it bother me, or I could let it roll off my back. No matter what anyone thinks, I am proud to embrace both Filipino and Polish cultures even though I don't necessarily fit into either one squarely.

Sometimes, even traveling within your own neighborhood brings out identity-defining experiences. A few years after my trip to Malaysia with my dad put me on the path to self-reaffirmation of my mixed-race identity, I had been briskly walking through the streets of New York City, admiring how much I loved the city's energy and diversity. In this city where the air seems to always pulsate with the feverish ambition of thousands of people taking their own unique routes to success, I've always felt more alive.

I smiled to myself and was about to put on headphones to blast my own soundtrack and transform my walk into a movie scene in my mind. Out of nowhere, a white male who looked to be in his late 20s stepped in front of me and demanded my attention.

"Hey! Just wanted to stop you and tell you that you have such a cool look," he said with an overconfident smirk.

I stared back blankly, wanting to get on my way towards the restaurant where I was meeting my friend Michael for dinner.

"Thanks," I mumbled with a half-hearted smile as I stepped forward and continued walking. Catcalling and random interruptions were nothing new to me after having spent the majority of my college years in NYC, but nevertheless, these encounters were always uncomfortable.

Seemingly not taking the hint, the man continued to walk alongside me and tried to spark some small talk, asking if it was my first time in NYC. I brushed off his questions as I kept walking faster. My pulse quickened not from feeling threatened, but from feeling utterly annoyed. The man then abruptly asked, "What are you? Like what's your ethnicity?"

I stopped in my tracks, not able to hold back a disgusted, disbelieving look from taking over my face. My mind raced: *What was the point of asking that question? Is he trying to categorize me? Or even worse, fetishize me as a mixed-race person?* A lot of memes had emerged in recent years where the general Internet consensus seemed to collectively acknowledge that mixed-race people were generally better looking and also produced better-looking babies.

Narrowing my eyes and turning to face this man head on, I boldly threw his question back at him: "When was the last time a stranger came up to you on the street and demanded to know your ethnicity?"

His eyes grew wide with acknowledgment that he had misstepped, as he tried to defend himself. "Well, I'm just, you know, white, so it's not that interesting of an answer. But *you!* You look like you're half of something, like you could be something really interesting."

My jaw dropped at that answer. "You should take a moment to think about how weird of a question that is, and how wrong it is that you feel entitled to an answer just because you are curious about my appearance from running into me on the street. I don't owe any explanation of my identity to anyone, especially not a stranger. Please don't ever ask someone that question again."

My heels clicked on the pavement as I confidently strode away. Adrenaline was coursing through me, making me feel pumped that I had the guts to stand up for myself and prevent another person from just putting me into a box or category based on race. I hated the fact that this complete stranger had the power to make me feel self-conscious about how I looked, since people like him clearly could identify me as "different" even just from a glance across the street.

I took a few deep breaths to calm down from that frazzling encounter and tried to remind myself that I'm not obligated to justify my heritage to anyone and I don't owe anyone an explanation of who or what I am. At the end of the day, we are all just humans. Race, ethnicity, nationality, or any other aspect of ourselves does not make a difference. Asking someone to define themselves in some pre-existing category only serves to help the observer try to make sense of a world that is moving away from tightly boxed categories.

The next time a stranger asks me that loaded question, "What are you?", I will happily reply that I am human. And that answer will have to be enough.

Australia: You Are Who You Travel With

"As with any journey, who you travel with can be more important than your destination."

—Gossip Girl

The sea breeze carried Aussie accents into my ears and the humidity of the tropics blanketed my skin as I strolled down the Esplanade in Cairns, a town nicknamed "the gateway to the Great Barrier Reef." I was excited for these next three days of solo travel in Cairns.

I had just finished my semester abroad as an exchange student in Singapore, where I had crossed paths with hundreds of travel-loving, adventure-seeking international students like myself from all over the world. From New Zealand, to Japan, to Bulgaria, to Mauritania, the friends I made spanned the entire globe and expanded my mind through stories of their lives back home. Our casual conversations about varying costs of living, drastically different university application processes, unique national holidays, and cultural perceptions of success, all taught me that the parts of life I typically took for granted as "normal" can be incredibly different in other corners of the world.

These friends from around the world were the main characters in my mind's replay reel of adventures from the different Southeast Asian countries I had explored every weekend of the semester. Trying deep fried tarantulas in Cambodia and scrambling up a volcano at the crack of dawn in Bali would not have been the same with any other set of characters, as each friend brought a unique perspective and personality dynamic to our trips. Our interlaced memories bonded us through belly-shaking laughter, foreign food adventures, and local guides gone wrong.

But the semester had just ended and I had exchanged tear-filled goodbyes with these former travel buddies, hoping we would remain lifelong friends. Solo traveling for the first time in over a year now left me with an abundance of mental and physical space that felt unfamiliar after five months of traveling with a friend by my side at all times. I sighed and let the whirlwind of experiences, relationships, and realizations marinate in my mind.

Lost in my own reminiscence, the salty ocean air permeated my lungs and I smiled as the hot sun of a southern hemisphere December tickled my skin, slowly deepening the golden-brown tan that Southeast Asia had given me as a lasting souvenir.

Australia had been on my mind ever since first grade, when my teacher led us through a unit all about the "land down under." Learning about marsupials, the biggest reef in the world, minuscule spiders and jellyfish with the capacity to kill you, and aboriginal didgeridoos all sparked my imagination. The toilet bowl water swirled in the opposite direction and Christmas was more likely accompanied by Santa hats on the beach than white winter wonderlands. At that young age, Australia seemed not only "down under" but also upside down and backwards.

Every small detail of my first day in Australia filled me with joy: from the currency adorned with emus, kangaroos, and platypuses, to the sewers spray painted with labels reading: "This drains to the Great Barrier Reef." My childhood memories of *Finding Nemo* projected onto real life as I gazed out at the blue-green waters and imagined Dory and Marlin swimming beneath the surface.

I was overjoyed to be experiencing Australia firsthand after so many years of longing to visit, but pangs of loneliness and regret continued to bubble up whenever I realized I was making memories that no one else could reminisce about with me.

On my first-ever solo trip in Slovenia the year before, I sheepishly choked out the words: "Table for one" for the first time and learned to wine and dine the awkwardness that sat in the empty chair across from me. With just enough food, drink, and uncanny confidence, the awkwardness turned into a moderate sense of comfort.

By now, I had mentally overcome the self-conscious initial phase of solo travel when it feels like everyone is silently judging or pitying you for seemingly not having any friends. Instead of worrying about how others perceived me as a solo traveler, I welcomed the opportunity to set my own daily schedule, eat exactly where I wanted, abide by my own budget, and not have to align my travel plans with whatever was the lowest common denominator among a group of travel buddies.

However, as I wandered around the sun-soaked streets of Cairns on my first day, the loneliness of solo travel crept in around every corner as I watched couples laughing and friends taking photos together. As much as I welcomed spending time alone with my thoughts, I reflected on how trips with friends meant more photos, more conversations, more jokes, and ultimately more memories. When I was alone on days like this, my environment served as a pretty backdrop, secondary to the thoughts and self-conversations in my brain. When traveling with friends, I was more likely to actively process everything around me since observations about the environment became the focal point of all our conversations and thoughts.

Sharing tiny Aussie-specific highlights of my day—*trying crocodile & kangaroo meat! finding Vegemite in my hostel kitchen! signing up for a scuba diving trip to the Great Barrier Reef!*—on my Instagram and Snapchat stories felt like casting a fishing rod out into the void. I hoped that friends back home, even despite the 16-hour time difference, could nibble on these digital messages in a bottle to somehow share in my joys of the moment and travel vicariously with me. I yearned to share my experiences with other people, if only to make sure these moments existed somewhere beyond my own mind.

Up until that point in my life, solo travel had been more about relishing alone time and the independence of being the captain of my own ship, or rather, executive producer of my own itinerary. But I knew that many solo travelers met and became friends with other solo travelers rather than spending their entire trips by themselves. Having never done this before, I decided to stifle the shy side of myself and instead try to turn my solo trip into an opportunity to meet new people.

Walking past the piles of snorkeling and scuba diving gear that dripped saltwater onto the wooden deck, I took a seat near the bow of my Great Barrier Reef expedition boat and locked eyes with a fellow solo female traveler. The standard traveler's introduction ensued: *What's your name? Where are you from? What brings you here? How long are you traveling?* An eager introduction and a smile as warm as the Australian sun was enough to convince me that Patricia from Austria, who was solo exploring Australia for a few months, seemed friendly and interesting enough to be my new best friend for the day.

We mingled our way around the ship as it sailed out to the middle of the reef, floating over the thousands of species of fish, sharks, coral, and turtles that called this patch of ocean home. Like a snowball rolling down a hill, Patricia and I bumped into new friends who piled on to form a makeshift squad of travelers. Ben and Tom from Scotland and Grace from England joined us as we excitedly discussed the sensations and sights of our first-ever scuba dives in one of the world's most iconic underwater destinations.

As the sun grew tired of watching us get to know each other, the moon swapped in and my travel squad migrated from the boat to other nearby hostels for some drinks, laughter, and gawking at strangers drunkenly dancing on stage. Conversation flowed as easily as the champagne into our glasses as we shared our highlights of the day, swapped tips and observations about other cities in Australia, and learned about each others' backgrounds and future travel plans. For a chronically shy person like me, who once told her middle school Public Speaking teacher that she would prefer to stand in front of the class in silence rather than talk about an improv topic for three minutes, I felt like I had finally kicked down the walls that previously made solo travel daunting.

Traveling to a place by myself didn't mean I had to experience everything alone. Connecting with other fellow travelers and sharing my thoughts and experiences in real time, even if only for one day, was magical. Travel can bring together people who are all very far from home, to experience new places and sensations.

Even if our paths might never cross again, our collective memories would always be intertwined, featuring each other as the main characters. Rather than my memories living within my own head or as snippets on social media, I could know in my heart that a few other souls out there in the world could resonate with the feelings of wonder and serendipitous joy from time spent in Australia. I might have been solo traveling for a few days, but I felt anything but alone.

~~~

After my three days in Cairns, I boarded a flight to Melbourne by myself. I waved goodbye to the reefs and rainforests of tropical northern Queensland. As my domestic flight soared above the outback from one tip of Australia to the other, my brain marinated in a mixture of despairing anxiety and eager anticipation. My not-so-solo travel days hadn't been spent alone, yet they were still a stark contrast to the upcoming week, when I would be spending every second of the day with a boy from Ireland named Jack.

At the beginning of my semester in Singapore, Jack and I happened to both join a group of exchange students heading to the ArtScience Museum. I struck up a conversation about music and once we discovered we were both avid concertgoers, I knew there was a spark worth kindling. Having been to over 200 concerts myself, a love for live music was always the catalyst for me to deeply connect with someone.

Looking into music festivals in Southeast Asia led us to plan a trip to Hong Kong, and we soon found another music festival in Australia happening the week after our semester ended. We booked plane tickets and concert tickets, along with a week-long trip to Japan and Korea for fall break, before even a semblance of a relationship had started to form. Our common interest in exploring new corners of the world and discovering local music scenes had drawn us together as fitting travel partners.

After our first trip together, we started to occupy each other's free time and thoughts. I went from barely even understanding Jack's Irish accent to adopting his unique slang and phrasing into my own everyday speaking. I found myself ending questions with "yeah?" rather than "right?" and putting an unnecessary "like" or "so" at the end of my sentences. The strangeness of this Irish permutation of the English language became my new normal the more I spent time with Jack.

Fast forward to our final ten days together in Australia, and I found myself saying the words, "I love you" out loud to a boy for the very first time—fittingly at a music festival, the common thread that had brought us together in the first place.

I never had a relationship in college because I was never in the same place for more than five months at a time for three years straight. My erratic study-abroad and personal travel schedule made it difficult for anyone, including myself, to see a point in investing in anything long-term. Meeting Jack in Singapore, in a situation where we were both thousands of miles from our homes, was a serendipitous stroke of luck that pushed us to confront the peculiar concept of having a relationship with an expiration date: the day my return flight was booked to take me back to the opposite side of the world.

When I touched down in Melbourne in early December and met up with Jack, I saw the next ten days together as a blissful opportunity to spend every minute of the day with someone I loved. But I also knew each passing day was also a ticking time bomb counting down to the explosive date of December 21 when our homebound flights would send us hurtling off to opposite ends of the Atlantic Ocean with no clear path forward on when we would possibly see each other again.

Despite the impending end date, it felt special to savor every moment together and invest in present happiness, without longevity as a prerequisite. Being conscious of a finite amount of time made me appreciate every second together even more, because I knew there would only be so few left. The feeling was similar to the phenomenon of spending a semester abroad—knowing you only have a few months to enjoy a new place with new friends, you seek out every opportunity to make the most of this finite time. Time limitations encourage us to optimize, maximize, and be strategic about our time and intentions, which ends up being a positive even if the impending deadline may feel stressful at the time.

Throughout our time together in Australia, I coaxed my mind to not think about the ending and instead simply relished the moment. The mantra "it's not a goodbye, it's a see you soon" echoed in my mind, even though I knew a long-distance relationship or cross-country contact was just not feasible given our different paths in life and the complications of obtaining working visas in each other's homeland.

Today, when people ask me about my trip to Australia, I immediately gush about how I'm absolutely obsessed with the country. I often cite the adorable animals and the diversity in landscape as reasons why everyone must prioritize a visit "down under." But when I think deeply about why I love Australia, I have to grapple with the fact that it wasn't anything particular about my trip to Australia that made me love the country.

What I loved about Australia were moments like simply sitting on a bench with Jack, drinking Little Fat Lamb alcoholic cola and laughing, as cars passed by in the evening glow of a street lamp. The renowned Great Ocean Road, golden coastal cliffs, and striking pillars of rock above the waves don't stand out to me. Rather, it's the sound bite of Chinese tourists complimenting Jack's "tall hair," making me laugh and smile. Likewise, in Sydney, the Opera House and other famous landmarks are outweighed by one random evening where Jack and I walked along the coastline, got incredible pancakes as breakfast for dinner, and wandered across the Harbor Bridge with the glow of Sydney's skyline twinkling like fireflies in the distance.

My time in Australia was characterized by an overwhelming amount of love for the person I was traveling with, which made every location, restaurant, and street memorable not for the icons that they were, but for the memories and emotions they helped create.

Reflecting on my days in Australia with Jack made me realize that I can have a great trip objectively no matter who I'm with. But, the subjective fondness of my memories of any trip is dependent on the person I'm traveling with, not just the place.

The next time someone asks me about Australia, I'll think a little deeper before answering. Did I love Australia itself, or did I love the person that I traveled there with? My heart knows the answer before my mind.

The small moments that can only be experienced and appreciated with a travel partner are what make trips special, memorable, and unique. These moments aren't necessarily tied to a specific place. The place, itself, becomes characterized by the inimitable memories that are created by the people you travel with. My time in Australia taught me that it's not always simply where I go, but sometimes who I'm with that determines how fondly I'll look back on a travel experience.

Abu Dhabi: Redefining "Normal"

"At its best, travel should challenge our preconceptions and most cherished views, cause us to rethink our assumptions, shake us a bit, make us broader minded and more understanding."

—Arthur Frommer

Sometimes, cultural immersion begins at the airport, before you even reach a foreign destination. In those rows of uncomfortable airport lounge seats, killing time before boarding, you can learn a lot by paying attention to fellow passengers whose concept of "home" is different from yours.

Boarding a flight to a foreign country is always an interesting confluence of culture: this flight to the United Arab Emirates was a mix of Americans like me, who were embarking on a trip to the Middle East, and Emiratis who were presumably returning to their homeland after a visit to New York City.

I nudged my friends Tommy and Amy as I observed the passengers who filed into the waiting area as the minutes slowly ticked by until the first call for boarding the plane. My friends and I were dressed like most Americans at the airport—sweatshirts, jeans, and leggings were our airport attire of choice. We were a stark visual contrast to the Emiratis fully swathed in long flowing garments that covered them from head to toe.

"This is exactly why I'm excited to take this class in Abu Dhabi. I feel so bad that I don't even know what their clothing is technically called." My face burned a bit as I spoke my ignorance into existence.

"Oh, definitely, same. I'm excited to actually go there and learn all about the culture firsthand," Amy agreed.

When I decided to spend my winter break in the United Arab Emirates taking a course on Middle Eastern Cultures, Markets, and Strategies, a couple of my friends didn't quite get how understanding Middle Eastern culture was relevant to my daily life back in America.

Growing up in predominantly white and Christian suburbia had kept me in such an insular bubble. I had only ever read the word Muslim or Bedouin in textbooks or newspapers, but the ignorance of my youth didn't have to last forever. I could read as many articles online as I wanted, but there would be no better way to understand the nuances and traditions of religion and culture in the Middle East than experiencing life there myself.

On the flight, the small TV monitor on the back of the seat showed the route of the plane from NYC to UAE. There was an unfamiliar arrow, pointing in some direction outside the plane. From the magazine in the seatback pocket, I learned that the arrow was pointing to the *qibla*—the direction all Muslims pray towards, namely, Mecca. This visual tool was helpful for Muslims on the flight who would need to properly orient themselves to perform prayers facing the right direction, even while hurtling through the air in a metal tube for 13 hours. I hadn't even landed in Abu Dhabi and I was already learning new things.

Tommy, Amy, and I arrived at the Abu Dhabi airport at around 2 a.m. after a 7-hour layover in Amman, Jordan, where we had the opportunity to leave the airport on a visa-free program to explore a bit of the city and get a taste for Jordanian food with a full spread of hummus, *moutabel*, *labneh*, *falafel*, and *tabbouleh* served with pillows of hot pita bread that melted in our mouths.

In the massive Abu Dhabi International Airport, every surface sparkled as if it had been cleaned mere moments ago. Arabic letters danced across every airport sign with their whimsical beauty. Despite not knowing at all what the foreign letters meant, I appreciated soaking in the sight of non-Latin letters. On any trip, this immediate disorientation was one of my favorite indications that I was indeed far out of my comfort zone. Somehow, not even being able to read or pronounce something made me feel like the trip was already worthwhile, exposing me to a sensation I might never encounter back home.

At the airport, the familiar shape of the Burger King logo, with its yellow hamburger buns and blue circle with red text, caught my eye, even with the swipe of illegible red Arabic lettering across it. Later, I saw a Wendy's logo where the normally white-skinned, freckled, red-haired girl had been swapped out for a red-haired girl of a darker brown skin tone. In that moment, the global marketing and localization teams of these fast-food chains had unknowingly made a massive contribution to my feeling of cultural immersion. The details that we take for granted in daily life can end up feeling the most jarring when we see them altered to reflect local demographics abroad.

As we made our way through baggage claim, Amy and Tommy joined me in awe as we soaked in the splendor of the airport.

We bought ourselves some steaming cups of *karak* tea for an energy boost after our 2 a.m. arrival and settled into a booth near the airport entrance as our bodies and minds began to internalize the new time zone. Without even looking at the clock, the early-morning darkness was enough of a signal that we would have to wait a few hours until the shuttle service would transport us to our dorms at NYU Abu Dhabi. In typical college-student fashion, we had all procrastinated our first assignment for our Middle

Eastern Cultures class, so we spent those few hours diving into readings and articles full of essential background information about the country we had just arrived in.

After equipping myself with vocabulary from the readings, I looked up and glanced around to observe the airport lobby with renewed understanding. The women wearing long black *abayas* that swished around their ankles and the men dressed in flowing white *kandoras* outnumbered the tourists in Western shorts and T-shirts. What struck me more than the difference in amount of exposed skin, was the difference in amount of exposed hair: nearly every man wore a red and white checked headscarf called a *ghutra* that covered their head, and the women covered their hair with black *hijabs*. I self-consciously wondered if my own hair was somehow offensive. As a girl growing up in America, I had often been told to cover up my legs or shoulders, but obscuring my hair and face was something that never crossed my mind.

In that bustling airport lobby, more impressive than the diversity in dress was the diversity in race and ethnicity. I noticed what seemed to be a range of South Asian, Southeast Asian, African, and Middle Eastern skin tones and realized for the first time that a country's claim of being a melting pot was in no way exclusive to America.

After a few more hours of people watching at the airport, we boarded a shuttle and made our way to the impressive NYU Abu Dhabi campus.

"Palm trees! Ok it's official, we made a huge mistake choosing the New York City campus instead of this one," Amy exclaimed.

Tommy and I laughed in agreement. It was January and we were sitting underneath palm trees and soaking up rays of sunshine.

This was already a striking departure from the post-Christmas gloom that tended to befall New York City as days grew dark by 5 p.m. and strangers hustled past each other on the street in parkas pulled up past their noses for warmth.

We soon met up with a dozen classmates who had also chosen to spend their winter break taking a class about the Middle East, in the Middle East. Strikingly, all of us were minorities ourselves. Although my classmates and I represented a great diversity of East Asian, Indian, Middle Eastern, and Latin American students, we lacked a single student of European or Caucasian descent. I wondered if this was pure coincidence or if it made sense that a more diverse population of students would be more curious to explore the culture of the Middle East. Perhaps it was a truth of life that identifying as a minority drives more curiosity about diversity.

"You may think I dress like this because I am Muslim, but our long garments and head coverings actually stem more from Arab culture than from religion!"

Jamila, our guide at the UAE Heritage Village, excitedly explained the origins of the clothing she was wearing. Her long black abaya brushed the floor as she led us through an exhibit showcasing the various styles of dress and face coverings that characterized the region and its citizens, both past and present. She had read my mind. I had assumed that any sort of long, body-covering robe was a religious requirement.

"I understand that many people think that the words Muslim and Arab are interchangeable, but not all Arabs are Muslims and not all Muslims are Arabs," Jamila continued.

She motioned to a painting of a traditional Bedouin camp in the desert. "We do not wear long robes and cover our heads and faces because we are oppressed. Part of why we dress this way is to honor our culture and how our ancestors lived. Covering up like this was essential to survival in the desert. Less exposure to the sun and protection from the winds and sandstorms are two key benefits of these traditional garments," Jamila explained.

"But isn't it hot in the desert when you're wearing so much clothing?" asked Tommy.

"The loose clothing actually is perfect for living under the hot sun! These garments shield our skin from the sun, and provide enough open, loose space between our bodies and the fabric that the heat is absorbed by the cloth instead of transferring directly to our skin." Jamila lifted her arms to demonstrate the amount of space and wiggle room there was beneath the fabric draped over her entire body.

"So, this clothing really does come from a basic human instinct for survival, not just a product of a religious belief system," I remarked.

"Exactly. Most Emiratis will wear an abaya as a way to connect to their identity, which goes deeper than just the religious aspect," Jamila smiled as she led us into the next room.

Drawing a line between culture and religion was something I never previously considered. Falsely, I previously thought of the Middle East as a mysterious monolith. Considering how the Middle East is portrayed with an overarching stereotype in most American media, I wasn't surprised that I was finding this nuanced understanding a bit mind-blowing.

From my reading, I knew that the population of the United Arab Emirates was almost entirely expatriates and immigrants, yet

Emiratis maintain a strong hold on their culture with the prominence of traditional dress as just one example. Though places like Dubai are more adjusted to tourists and not everyone abides by the suggested dress code, Abu Dhabi was less touristic and more likely to enforce the dress code. Wearing a full abaya wasn't a requirement, but tourists like myself were expected to wear long, flowy pants and minimize exposed skin in order to assimilate and not offend.

Jamila continued, "Many women around the world think that wearing a hijab or covering our bodies is a sign of oppression. But I don't consider myself oppressed. I make a conscious choice to preserve my own beauty and not sexualize myself for the benefit of men and societal expectations."

Oops. I had definitely made that mistake before. I made a mental note to never assume that a woman who wears a hijab has been forced into it. Learning that liberation can lie in the choice to cover up, or to not, was a new take on rejecting social norms and women's empowerment.

Later that day, my peers and I enjoyed a traditional meal while sitting cross-legged on carpets spread around the floor of a mud brick house. We tried on traditional clothing and I experienced firsthand what it might be like to cover my entire face except for my eyes. As I put on a *niqab,* which covered my eyebrows, nose, and mouth, I found it strange to think that covering these "beautiful" parts of the face was considered necessary for what some people deemed basic decency in this corner of the world. I had never thought that covering select parts of my face might be a way to avoid distracting men and to preserve a woman's beauty for herself or exclusively for her husband.

In my world of Western feminism, I had often heard that a free-thinking, empowered woman could wear as little clothing as she wanted and publicly flaunt her beauty through bold makeup and sexy outfits. Yet here in the Middle East, a version of female empowerment argued that a truly free woman kept her beauty and sexuality to herself, rejecting the need for external validation gained through showing herself off to the world.

Any empowered woman could decide for herself which version was right or wrong.

A few days later, my body weightlessly shifted from side to side as our 4 x 4 vehicle mimicked the motion of a roller coaster, speeding up and down the Al Khatim Desert toward a Bedouin-style camp. Everyone clutched their stomachs as the wheels of our Jeep kicked up sand with every sharp turn until we arrived at our destination in the middle of a golden sea of dunes extending in every direction.

Eager to exit the vehicle and to feel the stability of the ground below me after our nauseating ride, I kicked my shoes off and felt the warmth of the desert sand slowly envelop my skin. I tried to step out of my mind and be fully present in my body, to feel each individual grain against my sun-soaked skin.

The wind carried sounds of laughter from behind me and I turned around to see my classmates attempting to run up a sand dune for a better view of the sunset as it slowly made its way toward the horizon. The key word here being *attempting* to run. Trudging up a giant sand dune makes it feel as if every step you take only puts you further from your destination. My feet sank in deep as the sand gave way under my weight with each step and I continuously slid a tiny bit backwards, so each next step required greater effort than the last to make any progress at all. Frantically, I sped up my pace, kicking sand everywhere as I moved in place like running on a treadmill until a burst of energy finally helped me overcome the quicksand-like sensation.

The tough journey made the view from the top all the more worth it as my friends and I looked around at an unfamiliar landscape— nothing but piles of sand as far as the eye could see, bathed in the orange glow of sunset. I imagined myself in a ship looking out over an ocean, with the sand dunes shape-shifting into waves that seemed stuck in place. Thinking about how these dunes had withstood the test of time made me feel small and insignificant, in only the best of ways. I was a mere blip in the radar of all the creatures and people who had once soaked in this same view of the endless desert.

I ran my fingers through my hair and saw how much sand got caught underneath my fingernails from just this single action. As the wind picked up and tiny flecks of sand eventually covered every part of my body, the desert heat and wind made me wish I had the abundance of cloth from an abaya.

Once the sun winked goodbye over the horizon and the orange glow faded away, the sand dunes took on an eerie vibe. Where our feet had met warmth just under an hour ago, we now felt the coolness of each grain with each step as we descended the dunes and made our way to the Bedouin camp. There, we would spend the night watching belly dancers and listening to traditional music under the stars.

In most countries, grabbing coffee is simply a way to start the day with the necessary energy after a long night or early morning. But here, our outing for coffee was one way to experience the opulence and wealth that was so characteristic of the region. Ordering 24-carat gold-topped cappuccinos at the Emirates Palace was a memorable impression of the high standard of living in the UAE, thanks to its rich economy built on oil and tourism. This was opulence beyond compare; in no other place in the world is it a typical tourist experience to eat gold-leaf lined soft serve camel milk ice cream or get a latte sprinkled with 24-carat gold.

My awe at the extravagance of the country only grew as we visited the Sheikh Zayed Mosque, which was more impressive than any church I had ever seen. Even though I had been to dozens of churches all over Italy—the epicenter of Roman Catholicism and ornate cathedrals—none could compare to this most magnificent mosque that I consider to be one of the most impressive pieces of architecture in the entire world.

Walking up to this beacon of splendor whose white marble towers, domes, and hallways span the area of almost four football fields was a humbling experience.

White marble of the mosque glistened in the sunlight as if it were pristine, untouched snow. It was so clean and shiny that I could see my own reflection of wide eyes and mouth gaping in wonder beneath the blue fabric of my mandatory loaned abaya. Ornate carvings of flowers made of other precious stones and pure gold dotted the vast expanse of shiny white pillars and marble floors. The contrast of the white marble and the piercing royal blue in the reflecting pools around the mosque mimicked the blue and white of the sky and clouds, as if the entire world could be condensed and contained in this one awe-inspiring architectural masterpiece.

I basked in this imperial aura, feeling as if my childhood dreams of wanting to become a princess had finally come true.

As my peers and I slowly shuffled inside the mosque, every direction I looked inspired a greater sense of awe. Our necks craned back to admire the impressive ceiling featuring the largest dome and biggest chandelier in the world. Our feet were lucky enough to experience walking on the world's largest Persian rug, a modern wonder of the weaving world that took more than a thousand weavers over a year to complete. With each astonishing fact about the elements of the building and the records they broke, I grew to consider this mosque a perfect example of how humans continually try to defy expectations and accomplish the seemingly impossible. The United Arab Emirates was home to not only this record-breaking mosque but also the tallest skyscraper in the world. This country defied expectations, both in its architecture and its nuanced culture that held more to admire than to fear.

One wall stood out to me with six clocks each displaying a different time. I assumed that clocks like this represented different time zones around the world. However, this one clock actually reflected the sunrise, sunset, and daily call to prayer times that varied slightly each day, depending on the timing of sunrise and sunset. Once again, I was surprised by how many specific times of day were significant to millions around the world.

When we continued on and learned that women and men separated when praying, in different parts of the mosque, it made me more conscious of the fact that I indeed was a woman. This drastically contrasted my sense of self in America, where I tried as often as possible to forget my female differences and instead strive for equality in treatment. Much like wearing a hijab or an abaya made some women feel empowered, perhaps the separation during prayer made women less physically self-conscious during a spiritual moment. Though being treated differently under the rules of Islam based on my gender made me more aware of my gender and its role in my life, it also made me appreciate the freedoms that I formerly took for granted.

After a few weeks in the United Arab Emirates, my return to the United States felt like a return to newly appreciated freedoms. I could wear whatever I wanted, use curse words, diss my own government, and even kiss someone in public without risking imprisonment—all things that I had previously considered normal parts of everyday life not worth celebrating.

The things I considered "normal" were defined by how and where I grew up. Comparing my life to the lifestyle and customs I encountered in the Middle East served as a great example that "normal" is such a subjective concept based on your home location and personal experiences.

While I could now truly appreciate being able to do whatever I wanted in America, I also returned home with a tremendous appreciation for the cultural nuances and rules that make the UAE so special and unique. The country's customs are not "bad," and definitely not "weird"—just "different." While different is a statement of fact, weird or bad is a statement of judgment. With a greater understanding, through firsthand experience from traveling, I grew to appreciate the differences rather than being scared of them or feeling ignorant about them.

Argentina: Learning from Strangers

*"There will always be a reason why you meet people.
Either you need to change your life,
or you're the one that'll change theirs."*

—Angel Flonis Harefa

"Hola! Bienvenidos! Is this your first time in Buenos Aires?"

I glanced at my Cabify app to confirm my driver's name—Javier. He smiled at me through the rear-view mirror and I returned the gesture. Talking to local ride-sharing app drivers was one of my favorite ways to jump right into a local's perspective of their city when I arrived in a new country.

"*Si!* I've always wanted to visit Argentina." I excitedly rattled off my itinerary for the next two weeks: exploring Buenos Aires, heading up north to Iguazu Falls at the Brazilian border, down to the mountains of Patagonia on the Chilean border, then back to Buenos Aires to squeeze in a day trip across the river to Colonia Del Sacramento in Uruguay. Though Argentina itself is huge, I was thrilled about the opportunity to cross over multiple country borders and step into scenes of new food, dress, language, and culture even just for a day trip.

Colonial style buildings with rows of simple arched windows raced past my window in a blur of muted tan and warm clay colors. The European feel of the city center hinted at Argentina's history of colonization.

"Your country seems like it has everything! Two weeks hardly seems like enough time here, but I'm determined to make the most of it. I'm sure I'll find my way back someday to dive in deeper," I gushed to my driver.

"*Si, si*, we have many beautiful places to explore! Do you speak Spanish?" Javier asked.

"*Si! Yo sé un poco de español.*" My eyes lit up at the prospect of practicing a language that I loved in a country with a unique accent that made *Nueva York* sound like *Nueva Shork.*

"*Estudié español por muchos años en la escuela pero no puedo practicar recientemente.*" I stuttered out a few more sentences explaining how I had learned extensive Spanish in school but was very out of practice, as evidenced by my awkward word-on-the-tip-of-my-tongue pauses and improperly conjugated verbs. We rallied the conversation back and forth like a round of table tennis, with me answering his curious questions with significant focus and effort.

As the cab pulled up to my hostel, Javier gave me another smile and offered to connect on WhatsApp in case I wanted to book any discounted rides in the future without the fees from the app. Normally I would abide by the ride-sharing app's recommendation to keep all communication within the app for safety reasons, but something about having had a friendly welcome while practicing a language I love made me open to the offer.

A few hours and a few text messages later, I ended up spending my first evening in Buenos Aires trying local beers and empanadas with the taxi driver who had picked me up from the airport. I had absolutely zero romantic intentions and was purely seeking an opportunity to polish my Spanish and gain insights from a local, but as a solo female traveler I made sure to always be in a public place and not put myself in any undesired situations.

Javier practiced his English, and I strengthened my Spanish over the course of the conversation. My brain worked hard to conjure the correct words and phrases. Describing the wonders of my beloved New York City in an unfamiliar tongue forced my cognitive gears into overdrive as I attempted to distill the unique aspects of my city into basic vocabulary.

After a long conversation about local customs, job prospects in Buenos Aires, and Javier's dreams of one day visiting New York City, he severed a long pause with an abrupt interjection: "Can I kiss you?" I kindly declined and explained that I was traveling with a priority to figure out the world and figure out myself. Getting romantically involved with anyone was decidedly not one of my intentions.

My conversation with Javier was a striking reminder that as a female traveler who spent some days traveling alone, I was not only a tourist but a potential target in new locations. I wanted to believe it was possible to simply become platonic friends with locals during my travels. It felt disheartening at first to realize that I was often seen as a love interest rather than a source of friendship. *Did any guy ever want to just talk to me without some ulterior motive?* I asked myself in frustration. However, the experience was also an empowering reminder that I was in control of my situations and could still take advantage of opportunities to interact with locals in a way that felt safe to me. I had the power to say "no" and to set my own boundaries, deciding that a meaningful conversation could end there, without any further romantic involvement.

After saying an awkward goodbye to Javier, I descended the stairs to the underground platform and hugged my arms to myself while sticking close to the walls of the *subte* station. Riding the subway back to my hostel, I noticed the orientation of strangers who filled the train car. A few men were dispersed with entire rows of seating to themselves, yet the females gravitated toward the same clustered area. I realized it was an unspoken act of solidarity for solo women traveling home on the subway late at night to sit near each other. I reflected on my night and smiled at the women sitting near me as we silently scrolled through our phones, but simultaneously acted as a protective barrier for each other. Perhaps this type of local interaction was all I needed to feel a sense of comfort and connection in a new city.

After spending my first night in Buenos Aires grabbing drinks and talking for hours with my taxi driver, I recharged my batteries with a day of solo wandering through the streets and gardens of this verdant, vibrant city. As an extroverted introvert, I gained energy from alone time but also yearned to be with people. I only had to entertain myself for this one day. Tomorrow, I'd be meeting up with a friend of a friend who also happened to be traveling in Argentina during these same weeks.

Prior to agreeing over text message to spend the next two weeks together exploring the diverse landscapes of Argentina from north to south, Alice and I had only ever interacted in person by waving at each other from afar. Our mutual friend, Maddy, introduced us briefly one morning after identifying that we both had solo travel plans in Argentina coming up. We both decided that the transitive property applied to friendship: if we both got along with Maddy, then surely, we would get along with each other.

Still, the time I spent waiting for Alice to arrive at our hostel brought on the same swarm of butterflies in my stomach as waiting to meet a blind date. We'd already booked hostels, tours, and transportation together so if we happened to not vibe with each other, these next two weeks would quickly turn into a bout of awkward silences. However, the nerves quickly gave way to excitement as I thought about the adventures we had planned: admiring the world's largest system of waterfalls at Iguazu Falls, trekking across the Perito Moreno Glacier, and hiking a handful of the most scenic viewpoints in the Patagonian mountains along the border of Argentina and Chile. Knowing we were both eager to embrace the unfamiliar and seek out adventure, I was confident that we would quickly transition from strangers to friends.

Travelers always tend to be a self-selecting crowd who have more in common than those who are content to remain at home. I thought back to my randomly assigned roommates during my semester in Singapore—Ivana from Bulgaria, Carolin from Switzerland, and Bella from Colorado. Our upbringings may have been entirely different, but we had all opted-in to spending a semester living miles away from our comfort zones, traveling and meeting new people. This common desire to explore the unknown and embrace the cultural melting pot of Singapore tied us together more than any other common interest, TV show preference, or similar music taste.

The next day, I rocked on the stools in the hostel lobby, eagerly waiting to meet my new travel partner. A girl with a determined look in her eye and a big travel pack on her back walked through the hostel door. "Alice!" I exclaimed. Her eyes lit up in recognition as she walked toward me.

"Caitlyn! Sorry it took me forever to find my way here, I had a mishap with the airport shuttle," she explained.

After Alice checked in at the front desk, I guided the way toward our hostel dorm so she could set down her belongings.

"My flight only got in a day earlier than you, but I've explored Buenos Aires quite a bit already. Even had dinner with a local!" I hinted at my excursion with my taxi driver.

As Alice and I wandered around the greenery of Buenos Aires's expansive *Bosques de Palermo*, we quickly got to know each other and aligned on how excited we were for the activities and sights we had planned for the next two weeks of traveling. By the end of our first afternoon together, we were laughing and joking around as if we were old friends reuniting, rather than strangers hanging out for the first time ever.

In the early days of our trip, I realized that Alice and I had very different views on food. I highly valued trying local dishes while traveling, whereas Alice steadfastly adhered to a vegan diet for both health and environmental reasons. At first, sitting down at a vegan restaurant in the heart of a country known for its juicy steaks and sizzling *Provoleta* cheese skillets made me feel like I had made a dire mistake in agreeing to explore Argentina with Alice as my travel buddy.

However, as days passed and we had time to dive into deep conversations about her rationale for a vegan diet, I evolved to truly respect Alice's commitment to her health and the planet. In some areas of non-urban Patagonia, there were no vegan options whatsoever in restaurants, yet Alice still chose to only consume plant-based food items—resorting to simply raw nuts in desperate times. I admired her dedication and learned a lot from witnessing someone having such a steadfast commitment to their values, even when it got extremely difficult. We respected each other's food decisions and I grew comfortable going off on my own for a steak when I felt the Argentinian specialty calling me.

What Alice and I lacked in common food interests we made up for in common mindsets. We both approached each day of travel as an opportunity to prioritize learning and embrace novelty. One night when we ventured out to a live Latin American drum show called *La Bomba del Tiempo*, we met an Irish traveler in his late twenties who drunkenly whined, "Traveling is so unsustainable! There's so much drinking involved, I don't know how people can do this long term..."

Alice and I met his gaze with blank stares because we found his statement to be utterly unrelatable. To us, going out and drinking every night while in a foreign country was a choice, not an unsustainable inevitability. Prioritizing nature, culture, and uniquely local experiences made more sense to us than throwing away every evening and forgoing early morning starts for the sake of experiencing nightlife. Drinking and dancing tended to be fairly homogenous no matter where you were in the world, whereas landscapes, local cuisine, and regional history were location-specific.

Days later, Alice and I lived out our shared dream of trekking across the Perito Moreno Glacier in Patagonia. The sounds of the glacier calving and sending broken chunks of sparkling white-blue ice into the waters below reverberated through the air like thunder. Experiencing such a place of astounding natural wonder firsthand, and thinking about how it may cease to exist one day due to the damage we humans are inflicting on our planet, made me more inclined to do anything in my power to protect our beautiful world.

Spending time in the natural landscapes of Argentina, while observing and learning from someone like Alice, was a key factor in my mindset shift to prioritize plastic-free alternatives, conserve energy, and adjust to a largely plant-based diet. When I returned home from my travels, Alice's voice echoed in the back of my head, along with her recommendation to read a book called *How Not to Die* by Michael Greger. The book advocates for a plant-based diet, and was a main catalyst in my first attempt to adhere to a vegan diet for a few months.

Though we started out as strangers, my time with Alice in Argentina taught me that you don't have to have an extensive background or history with someone to feel extremely connected. The intensity of travel is able to supersede the tenure of years-long friendships. Alice and I had created more memories and shared more inside jokes from just two weeks together than I had with some people who I'd known for years back home.

When our time together came to an end, Alice excitedly suggested, "Let's make a list of superlatives!"

We sat down together and brainstormed some of the highlights and lowlights of our trip.

"Best hike?"

"*Torres del Paine* trek in Chilean Patagonia, for sure," I offered.

"Weirdest hostel?"

"That shack with the random rock-climbing wall!" We both laughed, remembering our confused faces when we first walked up to an unfinished wooden shack with a couch on the front lawn, which turned out to be our hostel for a night.

"Least vegan-friendly city?" I asked.

"El Calafate, ugh," groaned Alice.

"Most attractive unknown boy?" Alice and I both knew exactly who fit this superlative. We had no name to his face, but his physical attractiveness wasn't his only memorable attribute.

When Alice and I ventured to Iguazu Falls, we joined a tour group for the cross-border trip from Argentina to Brazil to see the famed waterfalls. Sitting across from Alice and I was a friendly-looking boy who spoke with a thick Argentinian accent. Before we even introduced ourselves or learned his name, the boy struck up a conversation about how he was from central Argentina in a sparse, rural region known as *La Pampa*. Though this was his home country, he was a visitor in Iguazu just like us, and it was his first time exploring the northern, more touristy region.

As we inquired about what it was like growing up in La Pampa, Alice and I were shocked to learn that he had recently moved all the way to Denmark to work in a hostel. Though being a hostel worker is not a particularly lucrative job, the striking difference in currency and cost of living between the two countries was the main draw. Earning a wage in Argentina's dwindling *peso* could not compare to earning high wages of Danish *krone* in a strong economy with a high cost of living. The purchasing power of a Danish paycheck could go exponentially further in Argentina with its comparatively low cost of living.

"There are no jobs in the countryside where I'm from," the boy explained. "I constantly had to worry about being robbed. But in Denmark, I feel safe every day."

He further explained to us how living in Denmark made him actually appreciate all that a government is supposed to do for its citizens. "I don't even mind paying taxes in Denmark! Every day I see construction and can be happy that the government is using our tax money to invest in essential infrastructure like bridges and roads."

"But in Argentina, you can never tell where your money goes, and life never seems to get better," he sighed.

I had never previously taken notice of how my government uses taxpayer dollars, nor had I ever considered working in a different country to drastically alter my earning potential. To me, taxes were just an obligatory part of life, not a connection between myself and a proactive, caring government. Feeling safe from crime was a constant in my life. I only ever perceived the presence of danger rather than notice and consciously appreciate the presence of safety. Hearing this boy's perspective made me more observant and thankful for the country that I had grown up in. I vowed to appreciate the safety and government accountability that I had previously taken for granted.

The boy shook our hands before departing the tour bus at the end of the day, and though Alice and I never learned his name, the perspectives he shared will linger in my mind longer than a name ever would have.

By reflecting on all the small moments that made our trip unique, I realized how many memories Alice and I shared. No one else would ever be able to take a trip to Argentina and experience these same moments through the same lens or perspective. The two of us, by some stroke of luck or fate, had chosen to travel to the same country during the same timeframe and had coincidentally shared a mutual friend who connected us.

I emerged from my two weeks in Argentina not only having a new travel buddy with many shared memories, but also a long-term friend whom I deeply respected and knew I could spend time with in the future. In fact, about a year after we first met, Alice and I both ended up moving to San Francisco after college to share an apartment while starting our first full-time jobs and exploring Northern California together. Traveling for two weeks and spending nearly every second of the day together in Argentina was the catalyst that turned a former stranger into one of my most valued friends.

There's a Japanese legend of an invisible red string originating from your heart and flowing out of your fingertips, extending to intertwine with the invisible strings of others whom fate dictates you are bound to meet. People like Alice, and many of the strangers I encountered on my travels, reminded me of this invisible string theory. Especially when traveling, you're bound to meet certain people who will transition from strangers to friends, or from strangers to teachers-in-passing, all while serving a role in opening your mind and prompting you to learn more about yourself along the way.

Antarctica: A Whole New World

"Look deep into nature,
and then you will understand everything better."

—Albert Einstein

Have you ever experienced true silence? Not just the absence of noise, but the presence of silence?

I first experienced this while snuggled up beneath multiple warm layers of clothing, in a waterproof sleeping bag, nestled into a burrow between two walls of snow in the middle of Antarctica.

I was six days into my Antarctic Expedition. Nearly a week had passed without Internet connection, cutting me off from any communication with friends or news from the outside world. Six hundred and twenty miles separated me from Ushuaia, the southernmost city in the world where I had boarded my Antarctic voyager ship. And that night, my isolation would hit its peak as I left the comforts of the 200-person-capacity ship and spent the night ashore with only a handful of other lucky explorers who won a lottery for the chance to open-air camp in Antarctica.

Earlier that day, my expedition guide, Benjamín, gathered our small group of campers on the deck of our ship to brief us on what to expect for the night ahead. As we settled into our seats, we gazed out at a parade of icebergs glistening in the sunlight. Benjamín tucked his dreadlocks under a large wool cap and sipped his *maté* from a thick thermos. The steam from his warm drink hovered in the frosty air, making me long for its warmth as the Antarctic breeze battered and reddened my exposed skin.

Benjamín turned to our small crew of Antarctic campers as he explained, in a thick Argentinian accent, "I've done this camping experience dozens of times now. I promise I'm not crazy, but truly we will not be taking any tents. It's just you, a sleeping bag, and Antarctica."

I glanced around me to affirm my own shock. Like myself, my fellow travelers had their eyebrows raised and heads cocked at an inquisitive angle.

Benjamín laughed, "Come on! Get those scared looks off your faces. This is your chance to be as immersed in nature as possible! It'll be worth it, I promise."

I had never even gone camping before, except in my backyard. And now I was just going to jump into possibly the most adventurous form of camping possible? *Everything's fine... growth only happens outside of your comfort zone, right?* I tried to hype myself up by thinking of the potential upsides rather than the potential discomfort.

"Meet back here in an hour. I'll start preparing the zodiac boats that will take us to shore."

My fellow passengers and I excitedly hustled back to our cabins spread across the tiny cruise ship. We had an hour to decide: what does one wear for a night camping in Antarctica?

After I suited up, three layers of socks, two layers of thermal long sleeves, double fleeces, a thick parka outer layer, beanies (yes, plural), gloves, and a thick scarf stood between me and the frigid outside world. My dad, who had taken the trip to Antarctica with me but had personally opted out of the camping excursion, looked at me in all my layers and laughed. "Did you get your fashion sense from the Michelin man?" he joked.

Before sending me off like a soldier to battle, my dad took a photo and stared at me with worrisome eyes as if he might never see me again—always the over-protective parent. I hugged him tightly and scurried off to the meeting point, practically waddling as the thick layers limited my mobility.

My heavy rubber waterproof boots thudded with each step as I approached the deck and shuffled into line to board the zodiac boats that would bring us to shore. One of these small, inflatable lifeboat-style vessels had already departed, carrying all the water-proof sleeping bags and layers of internal bedding that we'd rely on to survive a night beneath the Southern Hemisphere's stars.

One by one, the motorized zodiac boats whizzed across the water, piercing the stillness of the bay. I watched the silhouette of our big ship grow smaller and smaller against the bright horizon dotted with Antarctic islands as we approached land.

Once ashore, Benjamín navigated us to a flat area blanketed in un-touched snow with a picturesque view of the placid, dark green-blue Antarctic Ocean. To our right, a snow-covered mountain towered above us, its peak shrouded in a bank of gray, hazy fog. To our left, an expanse of snow dotted in brown emitted yelping noises every few minutes—a colony of seals!

Benjamín began narrating the logistics of the night. Maintaining the untouched, pristine state of the natural area was our number-one priority: "When we leave here tomorrow morning, it should look *exactly* like it does right now. You may have heard national parks use the phrase 'take only memories and leave only footprints' but here, let's try our best to not even leave traces of our footprints!"

One traveler piped up with the crucial question: "What do we do if we have to use the bathroom in the next 12 hours?"

Benjamín laughed and pointed at a toilet seat and bucket in the pile of gear we had taken ashore with us. "Your royal stool will be assembled shortly behind a pile of snow! Absolutely no 'going' in the wilderness."

The man who asked the question took in this answer with wide eyes and hesitantly nodded, perhaps willing his body to not need to relieve itself until we were back on our boat.

"We've got to carry in and out every single trace of ourselves to keep this place as free from human interference as it was before we got here," Benjamín explained. "Now, let's start digging ourselves a warm place to sleep!"

Following Benjamín's lead, our feet crunched against the icy, hard-packed snow as we fanned out and each selected a sleeping spot. Using a heavy shovel to dig out a hole in the snow that mirrored my body length, I felt like an animal preparing for hibernation. Despite my face growing red from the freezing temperature, I broke a sweat as multiple warm layers hugged my body.

Benjamín walked around our campsite, evaluating if each of us had dug deep enough. A tent may have been too difficult to stake in the ground, and wouldn't have held up against the brutal winds. But digging a hole deep enough to fully submerge your body beneath the snowbank for shelter from the wind was no easy feat either. My lack of upper body strength pushed me to toss aside the shovel and simply start kicking the snow out of the hole to burrow deeper.

"Don't be lazy! The burrow will allow you to harness the warmth of the snow. If you don't make it deep enough, the harsh Antarctic winds will keep you shivering all night," Benjamín warned.

I sighed and continued to struggle to dig an appropriate hole. When it finally looked deep enough for me to fit into, I inserted my waterproof sleeping bag as the finishing touch. Realizing I only had a few hours left until our early morning wake-up call to get back to the ship, I stripped off a few layers to prevent overheating and nestled into my cocoon of warmth beneath the snow.

As I wiggled into the sleeping bag, the snowy walls around me eroded small crystals of ice until I finally settled into a comfortable sleeping position on my side. The metallic silver lining of the sleeping bag reflected my body heat back at me, enveloping me in warmth despite the bitter cold. *Maybe this is what babies feel like when they're inside the womb. Or maybe this is what it feels like to be buried alive?* Lying in a ditch beneath the surface, with walls of snow encasing my body, was the closest I had come to sleeping in a coffin.

I yawned and watched my breath form clouds of water vapor in the crisp air. A few minutes passed with nothing but the sound of my own breathing forming its own meditative rhythm. Holding my breath for a moment, I paused and listened. *Silence.* The world was on pause. Nothing existed in that moment except my own thoughts. Even as the sound of my exhale filled my ears, the silence was still there.

Its stillness, its omnipresence, its peace brought isolation and the gift of self-reflection. Without anything else for my ears to perceive, I listened to the silence and stared up at the sky in disbelief. *I'm sleeping beneath the snow in Antarctica. Everyone I know back home has no idea what I'm doing right now. This is the most alone I'll ever be.*

Above me was nothing but endless white and brightness. I had to remind myself that it was nearly midnight, as the enigmatic midnight sun of the polar regions confused my body clock and chased away any hint of tiredness.

Eventually, I pulled my sleeping bag flap over my eyes to avoid being bathed in light. With the blinding bright sky and the complete absence of noise pollution, images of golden gates of light in the sky danced across my mind. *Is this what heaven feels like?* My mind continued to shuffle through different scenarios of what this experience could compare to, trying to pinpoint a description that accurately encompassed the feelings and sensations of this isolated serenity.

I drifted in and out of sleep, sometimes forgetting exactly where I was as I turned over in the sleeping bag in a half-awake state. A sound bite resurfaced in my mind of a podcast I had recently listened to, explaining how humans often don't sleep well in new places because half of our brain is in survival mode. If there were ever a time for my brain to be in survival mode, this was definitely it.

Glancing at my watch and seeing that it was nearly 3 a.m., I lifted the sleeping bag flap away from my face out of curiosity. The sky was still pure white. I squinted as I propped up on my elbow to peer above the walls of my sleeping burrow. Not even a shadow was in sight—everything was pure, unadulterated white. Brand new Crayola crayon white. Milky white. Fresh piece of printer paper white. This white couldn't even compare to any color I'd seen before. It was more a sensation of brightness than a perception of color.

Even when I shut my eyes, I still felt the brightness through my closed eyelids. I only had an hour until 4:15 a.m. rolled around and Benjamín would start waking us all up to pack and get back to the ship before it headed off to our next stop on the Antarctic peninsula. I tried to savor the sensations to crystallize a memory of this unique moment. White. Silence. Isolation. Peace.

Before a human-generated wake-up call could roll around, I woke to the sounds of whales singing in the distance. I imagined their graceful bodies gliding through the icy waters as they communicated to one another during their morning hunt for food.

The whale songs dancing over the icy morning breeze reminded me that though I was isolated and in the most remote location relative to other humans, I was anything but alone in the midst of Antarctica's natural population. Here, I was a temporary guest in a realm that belonged to the whales, seals, penguins, and even Antarctic midges, the tiniest forms of insect life on this desolate icy continent.

On previous trips, I had gotten up close and personal with monkeys in Cambodia, wallabies in Australia, and elephants in Thailand. I had spent weeks in national parks and mountain ranges across the globe, feeling immersed in nature. I've always strongly believed in the principles of leaving no trace. My dad often recounted the story of how my seven-year-old self stopped playing games during my school's field day to instead walk around the soccer field and pick up cans and trash that people had strewn across the grass. Even since that early age, I've been an advocate for our environment and knew that it was our responsibility as humans to keep our natural environment as clean as possible.

But camping in Antarctica was different. Litter was an obvious no-no, but until this camping trip I had never thought about the impact of leaving footprints or a trench in the snow. Benjamín had explained how our sleeping bag burrows could endanger the seals or penguins that might stumble into them if we didn't properly fill back in the snow. We came across a completely flat snowbank when we arrived here, and that's how we had to leave it.

My fellow Antarctic camping survivors and I rolled up our sleeping bags and began kicking down the piles of snow we had excavated while digging our burrows the previous night. We filled in the holes we had slept in to leave no trace of human impact, even in the inanimate snow. We brushed away the deep footprints left by our waterproof boots as we trekked out of the camping area. Though we may always keep the memory of camping in our own minds, the natural landscape didn't need a physical reminder of our camping experience.

This practice reminded me of the fragile balance we have with the natural world. So often, we humans take and take, and use a place for our own advantage. Realizing that I was a trespasser in the home of penguins and seals, I felt humbled by this experience. I knew, in the future, to put myself in the position of the other natural inhabitants of any environment I explored. Even if they couldn't speak for themselves to ask me to put things back how I found them, I knew now that it was always the right thing to do.

Spending a night sleeping out in the elements in Antarctica exposed me to the peace and silence that only true remote wilderness can bring. But, more importantly, it taught me the virtue of honoring the natural environment by being aware of my impact, even as seemingly inconsequential as digging a hole or leaving footprints.

Visiting Antarctica is probably the closest I've ever been to feeling like I had arrived on another planet.

Out of the roughly six dozen countries and the other six continents that I'd visited prior to Antarctica, remote wonderlands like Alaska and Iceland always ranked among my favorites. The stunning pristine blue and white color palettes of their crystallized glacial landscapes fascinated me and felt otherworldly compared to the beaches, forests, and cities of my other destinations. Something about exploring remote regions where humans shouldn't be able to survive, yet we do, sparked my intense curiosity. Antarctica was no different.

The majority of people who visit Antarctica, myself included, do have a goal of checking off the seventh and most elusive of the world's seven continents. But, most importantly, I wanted to visit because Antarctica is one of the most unique places on Earth that could push me the furthest out of my comfort zone and teach me the most along the way.

A trip into the relatively unknown allowed me to satiate my yearning for adventure by traveling to some of the world's most remote places while meeting some of the most adventurous, travel-loving people out there and viewing my favorite animals, penguins, in their natural habitat. Visiting Antarctica was a win-win-win for me as a trifecta of exploring a vastly different terrain, meeting interesting and like-minded people, and experiencing peak cuteness during the time of baby penguin hatching season.

A few days before my polar camping experience, I had embarked on an Antarctic voyage across the Drake Passage aboard the Polar Class 6 *Hondius* expedition cruiser that could sail through 4-foot-thick ice. Any knowledgeable captain will tell you that the Drake Passage is home to the roughest seas in the world, separating the tip of South America from the Antarctic peninsula. Our captain had told us horror stories of previous voyages where waves taller than a five-story building would rock the 200-person capacity boat like a young child violently rocking a baby in a cradle. On turbulent nights like this, drinks had to be weighted down to the tables; otherwise, they would fly off and smack into the windows on the opposite side of the ship's dining room.

However, we got lucky with an exceptionally fast and smooth voyage across the Drake Passage. One of the tour guides on our Antarctic adventure crew remarked, "You're so lucky you got the Drake Lake, rather than the Drake Shake!" Despite our apparently lucky and relatively calm voyage, I would still say my experience on a rocking boat in the Drake Passage is the closest I've ever gotten to a feeling of weightlessness and an utter loss of center of gravity.

On multiple prior trips on conventional cruise ships, I had never before gotten seasick. Yet while crossing the Drake Passage, my stomach protested constantly as the ship rocked side to side for the 48 hours that it took to sail from the tip of Argentina down to the shores of Antarctica. Along every staircase and corridor, I steadied myself each step by grabbing the railings that were adorned with white paper bags in case anyone spontaneously felt the need to part ways with their last meal. The rocking of the Drake made any sober passenger look like they were four drinks in as they wobbled down the ship's narrow hallways.

In any normal situation where I had 48 hours to kill while in transit, I'd usually turn to my phone as a source of entertainment and connection with friends back home. However, there was no cell service on a boat in the middle of the Southern Ocean. Most people in our increasingly digital world can't imagine ten days straight without a single Google search, text message notification, or scroll through a social media feed. But during my Antarctica trip, I enjoyed the forced disconnection. I discovered that yes, a digital detox can do wonders in allowing you to be fully present while traveling, and no, your social life will not suffer if you miss out on friends' updates for a few days. I nestled into a window porthole to read wildlife handbooks and physical encyclopedias for hours on end, reveling in the fact that no one could reach me even if they tried.

The ship's expedition crew became my real-life Google search engine. Their expertise filled the two days of sailing across the tumultuous seas with engaging lectures that helped us all keep our minds focused on something other than our rocking ship. The Antarctic expedition guides were not only trained in piloting zodiac boats, navigating glaciers, and interacting with penguins, but also were PhDs across a variety of fields like glaciology, geology, and marine biology.

I had signed up for a trip to Antarctica, but ended up getting a crash course on how glaciers form, how to identify different penguins and seals, the politics of the Antarctic Treaty, and the dangers of ocean plastic in the Antarctic. The average tourist might not want to spend their vacation attending lectures, but Antarctic explorers were not average tourists. The room was packed for every lecture, as we all were eager to learn for the sake of learning. As a fresh college grad who thought she had just said goodbye to classrooms forever, I was actually ecstatic to be back in learning mode. I enthusiastically soaked up all the information, not to pass a test or to prove my intellect, but to give myself a greater understanding and appreciation for the Antarctic environment.

My dad and I spent the two long days at sea alternating between attending the guides' lectures and staring out at the endless ocean from the back of the ship. We watched giant albatrosses use their massive wingspans to float over the frothy wake of the ship rippling across the dark, green-indigo ocean. In the evenings, we gathered in a dining hall where we rotated on an open seating plan to meet and dine with the other passengers and Antarctic expedition guides. I loved sharing a meal with the guides and hearing about their exciting lives, spending half their year exploring this continent that hardly anyone in the world actually gets to see.

These conversations planted the first seeds in my mind that maybe I should abandon my typical life and standard career. Maybe I should just go rogue and spend my days as an expedition guide, experiencing the wonders of Antarctica for the first time over and over again through the fresh eyes of new travelers. It was the first time I felt like studying business had been a waste. My knowledge of financial accounting and the 4 P's of marketing could not stack up against the practical life skills of knowing how to survive and ensure others' safety in one of the most brutal natural environments on the planet.

When our ship finally emerged from the menacing Drake Passage and we could once again walk in a straight line without stumbling, we had more than one reason to celebrate. We had survived a journey across the world's roughest seas. We could finally see the landmass of Antarctica on the horizon. And it was New Year's Eve!

My 2020 started out on a small but mighty vessel in the middle of the Southern Ocean with nearly 200 strangers from a collection of 27 different countries. With no Internet connection to pull us away or distract us with New Year's wishes from our friends and family scattered across various time zones, my fellow Antarctic explorers and I lived fully in the moment as we crowded onto the bow of our ship, sipped mulled wine, and danced beneath the endlessly bright sun as the clock struck midnight.

We were all united for that moment in the long-term excitement of new possibilities for the new year ahead, and the short-term anticipation of exploring Antarctica's unknown wonders the next day. No matter if we ever crossed paths again, we would all share this unique collective memory of starting the anomalous year of the COVID-19 pandemic in the most unconventional way possible—floating amidst a sea of icebergs, mere miles away from Antarctica, underneath the sun that never set.

Whenever I say "I took a trip to Antarctica," the reaction to this claim usually ranges from disbelief to jealousy to confusion. Some people, who think Antarctica is impossible to reach, think I'm joking; others, who aware of the prohibitive cost and intense planning process to visit the White Continent, are wildly impressed; and others, who consider a big freezing chunk of ice to be an unappealing vacation destination, are confused why I would go out of my way to visit in the first place.

One of the main draws of visiting the remote wilderness of Antarctica is the opportunity to view penguins in their absolute natural habitat, hundreds of miles away from any human development. Only around 50,000 people—less than 0.0006% of the entire world's population—travel to Antarctica each year, making it truly one of the most remote, untouched opportunities to experience wildlife in its most natural form.

I was absolutely captivated not only by the endearing waddling of penguins shifting their weight from side to side while holding their flippers out for balance, but also by dozens of penguins gracefully gliding in and out of the water in unison in a method known as "porpoising," just like a dolphin briefly emerging from water as it glides through the ocean.

My time in Antarctica during early January coincided with prime penguin hatching season. Witnessing tiny penguin chick beaks *peck, peck, peck* and finally break through the outer layer of their shells to see their first-ever glimpse of the world brought salty tears to my eyes that almost froze to my cheeks.

In addition to this precious start of life, I also witnessed the potential end to it soon after, as a predatory skua—a bird that eats penguins—swooped down into the penguin rookery and repeatedly dove at a newborn chick, trying to pick it up with its beak until an adult penguin furiously waddled over to chase the predator away. Bearing witness to this circle of life in raw form, playing out right before my eyes, made me realize how no artificial zoo encounter with wildlife could possibly compare.

I'll never forget being on a small zodiac boat drifting through a sea of icebergs, the fog so thick that we couldn't see our ship in the distance, when a humpback whale suddenly surfaced merely a few feet away. In a majestic arc of its body, this massive creature that spanned the length of two school buses breached the surface with more grace and coordination than the most classically trained ballerina. The spectacular few seconds between emitting spray from its blowhole and kissing the surface goodbye with a gentle flick of its fluke was mesmerizing. This creature, so large that our zodiac boat felt like a toy in comparison, had the capacity to kill us, but instead just let us stare in awe and wonder at its beauty and majesty. I felt small. I felt humbled. I felt rightly put back in my place—humans are not the kings of the earth we so often make ourselves out to be.

Watching a creature like the baby penguin struggle to survive in its own natural habitat versus seeing the humpback whale utterly dominate the ocean with its size and authority had a grounding effect. I felt more connected than ever to the natural world, and knew my place in it. Immersing myself deep in the remote natural wilderness of Antarctica made me feel a deep sense of gratitude for the extraordinary opportunity we all have to make the most of our lives before we are subjected to the whims of Mother Nature.

Staring out at one last sparkling, untouched sheet of ice after our ship had begun our journey home away from the White Continent, a conflicting mixture of gratitude and guilt swirled in my mind. Should I even be here? What right do we have to enter this remote wilderness just to satisfy our personal curiosity?

I debated with myself, remembering the strict procedures for biosafety we followed to ensure no invasive species were brought to Antarctica. I thought about the strict distance rules of staying at least 15 feet away from wildlife unless they choose to approach you, to ensure that we are not causing stress or negative influence to the animals.

A sound bite from our expedition guides' lecture on the politics of Antarctica resurfaced: "You are all now Antarctic Ambassadors. Most people aren't motivated to protect a place they've never seen themselves, so now it's your duty to spread your love for Antarctica when you return home." As much as Antarctica provided me, I now was responsible to give back with my own future actions.

Antarctica was now a part of me. In 2041, when world governments will vote to renew the treaty that preserves Antarctica by prohibiting drilling and extractive industries, I will proudly assume my Antarctic Ambassador duty. My photographs, stories, and memories will help me influence my communities to support preservation of this place that is not just a hulking chunk of ice in the Southern Ocean, but an alternate universe of sparkling ice caverns, whales, and penguins that taught me the servant role we humans need to have in our environment.

Kenya, Tanzania, and Malawi: Life on Safari

"There is something about safari life that makes you forget all your sorrows and feel as if you had drunk half a bottle of champagne—bubbling over with heartfelt gratitude for being alive."

—Karen Blixen

"Caitlyn! Wake up, there's something outside our tent!"

The sound of my own name jolted me awake as I quickly tried to remember where I was. I turned to see my travel buddy, Maddy, cowering in her sleeping bag with her head turning from side to side, trying to determine exactly where the animal noises were coming from. Camping out in the middle of the vast, endless plains of the Serengeti in Tanzania put us squarely in the middle of the African wilderness, with nocturnal creatures making their nightly rounds.

I was halfway through a seven-week camping safari with a group tour that was designed to travel overland via truck, starting in Kenya and meandering through Tanzania, Malawi, Zambia, Zimbabwe, and Botswana before ending in South Africa. This trip had sounded like a once-in-a-lifetime opportunity to cover a lot of ground, get as close to nature as possible by camping nearly every night, and stay within a reasonable budget. However, as the weeks went on, I discovered how truly mentally unprepared I had been to dive head first into this experience that put me miles away from my comfort zone—both physically and mentally.

Just a few short months prior to this trip, I had never even heard of the concept of "overlanding"—a mode of travel quite common for those who want to explore large areas of land on a budget, often in countries or regions that have not yet built up networks of hostels and budget travel options for the do-it-yourself backpacker. Europe and Southeast Asia have reached a saturation point of tourism where there's an endless array of cheap and conveniently located hostels, budget airlines, and overnight bus networks to cater to the adventurous solo traveler or group of friends looking to explore the region. But East Africa is a whole different story. Since the highlights in each country tend to revolve around nature and game reserves full of wild animals, the locales of interest tend to be remote and difficult to navigate between. Having a local guide and a trusty big yellow truck as a reliable mode of transportation was key to a smooth trip.

Thanks to the expertise of local guides and well-planned safari routes, we wrapped up an unbelievably lucky first week on safari, having spotted the "big five" iconic safari animals—lion, elephant, rhino, leopard, and Cape buffalo—at the Lake Nakuru and Masai Mara National Reserves in Kenya. Along with the full nature experience, we had an opportunity to immerse ourselves in local culture during a stay at Maji Moto, a village that is home to a Maasai tribe. We learned how tourism income from this cultural camp helped fund a boarding school for Maasai girls who were rescued from traditional villages around Kenya that practiced female genital mutilation. Knowing that our campsite fees were creating a positive social impact, we set up our tents and slept easy as Maasai warriors wearing red capes stood guard overnight to ward off any lions. Just one week in, the safari life had blown away my expectations like a fragile leaf swept away by a gust of pure awe.

Our big yellow truck rolled out of Kenya on a high note as we entered Tanzania, a woefully underrated country that has everything an adventurous traveler like me could possibly look for. As a lover of hiking, I took a day trip to trek to the first base camp of Mount Kilimanjaro, the tallest free-standing mountain in the world. After yearning for the beach during the past few weeks of overland safari life, I wandered the idyllic white shores of Zanzibar Island while watching dolphins play in the tropical waters of the Indian Ocean. A longtime lover of history and anthropology, I visited Ngorongoro Crater and the Cradle of Humankind. The animal lover in me vowed to come back and time my trip right to witness the annual Great Migration of over two million wildebeest, zebras, gazelles, elands, and impalas across the Serengeti plains.

On our overnight stay in the middle of the Serengeti, our local guide had warned us that our campsite, though designed for human inhabitants, was not gated off in any way, so it was possible for any intriguing smells to draw in some animal visitors overnight. We were in the heart of the animal kingdom—the lions, elephants, cheetahs, leopards, wildebeests, and more were the rulers here. We were mere visitors, enjoying temporary permission to explore their domain.

After Maddy's abrupt, fear-induced wake-up call, my mind raced, trying to think of what objects in our possession might be emitting even the faintest smell to attract a curious, hungry animal. We had heeded the advice to store all snacks, food, and even minty-smelling toothpaste in our safari vehicle in order to make our tent as unattractive to animals as possible. Perhaps Maddy and I had gotten too caught up in staring at the blanket of shimmering stars above our campsite, here in the Serengeti's sky devoid of all light pollution. As we stared up at the sky until our necks hurt from leaning back for so long, we may have forgotten a scented bar of soap somewhere in our backpacks.

Despite the darkness of our tent, I made eye contact with the whites of Maddy's eyes. Both Maddy and I remained motionless, to prevent our synthetic sleeping bag material from making noise. The sniffing grew louder and felt like a more immersive experience than any surround-sound TV. From the sniffing, we could tell the creature was taking a lap around our tent.

My mind immediately flashed the worst-case scenarios: a lion on the prowl? A family of hungry cheetahs? Or worse, a hippo, which I had recently learned held the title of world's deadliest land mammal, killing more humans per year than any other animal in Africa.

We started to hear whimpering, like a cross between the sound of a baby gurgling and the *ooo oo ooo*'s of a monkey—the language of laughter only a hyena could produce. More rustling a bit further away seemed to indicate a pack of hyenas, and we realized these scavengers of the plains must have found a way to topple the nearby metal garbage can. Beyond the obvious animal noises, we couldn't help but laugh at the snores of one of our fellow travelers, which could almost be mistaken for the purr of a cheetah had we not already known our safari group contained a chronic snorer.

Maddy and I were frozen in rigid trepidation as we waited for the rustling, whimpering, and occasional howling to subside. The fact that we couldn't confirm our suspicions because we didn't want to emerge from our tent and put ourselves in danger only added to the anxiety. Somehow, our adrenaline eventually fell victim to exhaustion and we drifted off to sleep.

Waking up in the middle of the night to the sound of hyenas sniffing our tent, and being inches away from these fierce hunters that could mistake us for their next meal, was definitely something I never expected to happen. But, it ended up being my most illustrative example of how deep we were in the heart of the wilderness on this unique camping safari experience.

As our safari Jeep traversed the endless plains of the Serengeti the next day, I turned to Maddy as we both stared out the window at the horizon in awe.

"If anyone wanted to convince me the world was flat, all they would need to do is take me to the Serengeti," I said, in near disbelief.

"It's actually unreal!" Maddy agreed. "We've been driving around for hours and there's not even the tiniest bit of elevation in any direction."

"No wonder this is such a great spot for seeing animals. There's nowhere for them to hide!"

During our drives in the safari game reserves, we quickly got used to a new set of road rules and expectations. Rather than yielding to pedestrians, we yielded to flocks of guineafowl, the African chicken lookalikes whose red and blue heads bobbed back and forth as their white-spotted bodies hurried across the dirt roads.

Back home in the suburbs of New York City, I'd often see deer on the side of the road where I now had grown used to seeing warthogs and gazelles prancing through the plains. Instead of stopping at human crosswalk signs, we stopped at elephant crossing signs. Forget slowing down when driving behind a bulky truck back home. On safari, we had to slow down when driving behind a lion lazily slinking its way along the dirt road directly in front of us.

At times, this close human and animal contact gave me pause. Was it wrong for us to encroach upon these animals' homelands, simply to gawk at them and snap photos? Were we, the tourists, the sole benefactors in these close wildlife interactions? This guilt ate at me, especially at times when a crowd of safari vehicles would all gang up together whenever a rare animal, such as a lion or rhino, was spotted hiding amidst the grassy terrain.

I was relieved to learn from local guides who conduct safari tours for a living that tourism is actually essential for the survival of animals in these regions. Local governments often cannot dedicate money to fund anti-poaching programs in order to keep the animals safe without tourism income. If local families were unable to generate income through tourism, they themselves would most likely resort to poaching, since it is the only other viable source of income on a scale comparable to tourism.

It surprised me to learn that tourism is a solution often praised by conservationists. I pictured the animal-abuse picket signs and protests during my childhood visits to the circus, and had assumed anything but leaving animals to their own disposition in the wilderness would be criticized by animal rights activists. In an ideal world, poaching could be stopped altogether and we wouldn't need tourists to fund the maintenance and patrolling of conservation areas and national parks. But in the current reality, this symbiotic link between tourists and animals, who depend on one another for enjoyment and survival, respectively, will always stick with me. Humans are simultaneously the problem and the solution to environmental issues.

The next few weeks of life on safari passed by in a blur of wild-life encounters, long drives, and late-night talks with my fellow travelers. Nearly every day, we rallied our tired bodies to wake up before dawn after occasional sleepless nights when sounds of baboons and hippos kept us awake. What made the early morning wake-up calls worthwhile was catching the first glimpses of sunlight peeking through the morning clouds. A kaleidoscope of deep pinks, fiery oranges, vibrant yellows, and soothing purples was often our backdrop as we packed ourselves into safari vehicles and set out for game drives during the early morning hours when animals were most active.

Bearing witness to the everyday happenings of the animal kingdom in a firsthand setting felt like I had crawled inside the National Geographic documentaries that lit up my TV back home. One minute, we watched a family of cheetahs feasting on an unlucky impala, the blood splatters on the cheetah cubs' fur shining like badges of honor as they mimicked their mother devouring the prey. The next minute, we stumbled upon a lion and lioness in the midst of the act, procreating the lion heir that would one day rule everything the light touches, just like Simba from the Lion King. Other days, our safari truck would turn a corner and we'd suddenly lock eyes with a leopard, a most elusive savannah inhabitant, as he stared down at us from a low tree, with the remains of a warthog slung over the tree branches.

Our safari's opportune timing of mid-February meant it was baby-animal season, and we were not disappointed, eventually spotting nearly every type of adult animal accompanied by smaller silhouettes. Newborn warthogs, hippos, cheetahs, leopards, elephants, and more, melted our hearts and filled us with fuzzy feelings of adoration.

On the days we weren't exploring animal habitats, we set out on long drives. Sometimes driving up to 10 hours straight in one day was necessary to traverse the nearly 3,000 miles down the southeast African coast from Kenya to South Africa. During these long drives, I rekindled my love of reading. Throughout my college years, I always told myself I had no time to read for pleasure. There was always a reading for school that I could barely even fit into my busy schedule, and the thought of doing things for pure leisure that wouldn't either be extremely fun or extremely beneficial to my professional life didn't seem worth it. The ghost of comparison haunted me as I thought that every second I didn't spend doing something productive, someone else who had my same goals and dreams *was* doing something productive—they would get ahead, leaving me in the dust.

However, during this extended safari trip, after I had graduated and already secured a full-time job, I finally felt an inner sense of peace. There was nothing left to compete for. No obligations were weighing me down. I could read a book about a topic that interested me purely because I wanted to, and I didn't even have to tell anyone that I did.

Relearning how to read for the sake of enjoyment and not for personal or professional development was one of the small joys of safari life. Because I was captive on our safari truck for full days at a time, often without any Wi-Fi or cellular data that could have kept me mindlessly scrolling for hours, I was able to settle down with a good book for hours on end for the first time in years, and truly enjoy something I had previously convinced myself was an unnecessary waste of time.

Another perk of having spotty Wi-Fi service was the fact that during our dinner conversations, everyone was fully present as we sat in a circle around a campfire, underneath the stars, eating food we had just cooked ourselves with a makeshift camping stove. Never did we have to worry about an incoming notification stealing someone's attention away from the conversation, and for that reason, my safari camping group and I were able to develop deep connections and bond with each other in an extremely condensed time frame. We spoke of future dreams, scars from our past, relationships gone wrong, trips gone right, and our collective daily astonishment and gratitude for the incomparable safari life we got to experience every day.

If I ended this story here, you might be led to believe that every day on safari was nothing but once-in-a-lifetime wildlife interactions, fulfilling self-reflection, and connecting with fellow travelers and the world around us. As much as I appreciated these special moments that elevated me to previously unimaginable highs, my life on safari as a whole would not be complete without the low points.

"THIS IS MISERABLE!!!"

"I'm covered in tiny dead flies."

"Can't do it, just can't do it anymore."

These stream-of-consciousness notes scrawled into my travel journal reek of desperation and defeat. It was five weeks into my camping safari journey and my first night in Malawi—a fairly small, land-locked country in southeastern Africa that is off the beaten path for most travelers. Five weeks in austere conditions was trying, and things were not going according to plan.

I sat cross-legged on my sleeping bag inside my tent as tears mixed with the layer of perspiration that coated my body in the nighttime humidity, characteristic of a country in the tropics. Our campsite happened to be next to a lake, which was the root cause of all my problems and discomfort that evening. Close proximity to a body of water meant this was a fertile breeding ground for bugs like the African lake flies, or midges, that emerge during the new moon in the rainy season.

When I say there were little flies everywhere, I truly mean *everywhere.* We were lucky that we had a tent that was designed to be mosquito-proof, with a tightly sealed zipper entrance, but even just the hour we had spent outside the tent assembling it was more contact with the tiny little flies than I could bear. And that was before dinner.

It was late in the evening, so a single light bulb hanging from a small hut illuminated the area where we assembled our small foldable stools in a circle for our nightly ritual of scooping homemade basic meals out of the makeshift pots into our reusable containers and plates that had traversed the African continent with us over the past few weeks.

I glanced up at the sole light bulb illuminating our eating area, and I couldn't even see the lightbulb itself. Swarms of tiny little flies had surrounded the bulb, looking like a sandstorm. Hundreds more circled around every light source in sight.

In any other campsite, I would have been delighted to find that the outhouse toilet was lit with a lightbulb, but here it was a trap. I would rather pee in the dark and potentially run into hidden spiders and creepy crawly bugs than deal with the lightbulb inviting the attention of hundreds or thousands of tiny little flies. I couldn't even think about brushing my teeth and providing an opportunity for the midges to enter my mouth. If I had to go to sleep with plaque on my teeth, rather than tiny flies, that seemed like a bargain I was willing to take.

No matter how much I swatted at my face, or how much bug spray I applied, the flies just kept coming, seemingly on an intent mission to fill any and all of my air holes with their incessant buzzing and flapping of their tiny little wings. After transcribing my frustrations into my travel journal, I flopped onto the folded-up sweatshirt that I used as a pillow while camping. I tried to bury myself in my sleeping bag, hoping that sleep would supersede the frustration and despair clouding my mind.

Even the past 48 hours before the midge-infested campsite in Malawi had been a series of unfortunate events that continually eroded my optimism and enthusiasm. First, the overland truck that we had been traveling on broke down and we had become stranded in southern Tanzania for nearly 24 hours.

During this miserable day and overnight period, we had zero Wi-Fi connectivity, no local money to buy anything, and, most crucially, no air conditioning: a perfect storm for time to feel like it was moving as slow as humanly possible. When someone in my travel group remarked, "Did you all realize it's leap day today? I guess this day doesn't exist after all," it felt like some weird Twilight Zone occurrence where the day neither existed in reality nor in most years' calendars.

Our group of mostly white tourists stuck out in this small town seemingly in the middle of nowhere. Everywhere we walked, the murmurs of locals calling us *mzungu*, the Swahili word for white people, made us feel even more othered and out of place. Times like these made us reflect on how far we were from home and how unexpected our situation was.

On that day of nothingness, it was easy to sink to the bottom of the sea of negative emotions and focus on everything that had been frustrating and disappointing. Though some days blessed us with beautiful temperate weather, other days and nights were unbearably humid, driving us to decide if we would rather remain in our hot box of a tent, or sleep outside in the cooler night air and risk getting malaria from the mosquitos. On some days, we encountered nothing but rain—a nonstop, miserable type of rain that made us curse the band Toto for writing their iconic song.

There were the times when our local guide would deliver the devastating news that the next campsite had no running water, and we all had to reckon with the reality of at least another day existing in yesterday's skin soaked with sweat, sunscreen, bug spray, and the dirt and dust from a day of driving through the African plains. When we were lucky enough to have running water, and even sometimes the absolute luxury of *hot* running water, we had to be sure to shower before nightfall. The darkness would bring out mosquitos that threatened to feast on our skin in the most inopportune places as we scrubbed the layers of dirt off our naked bodies.

On safari, I'd sometimes rather wish I were dead than have to deal with getting out of my tent in the middle of the night and walking a few hundred yards away through cold, dew-soaked grass, to simply relieve myself. The daily struggle of not having proper access to a toilet even drove me to drink less water, just to deal with these unfortunate bathroom situations less often. Another key reason to limit water intake was that any running water we encountered in a sink was likely unfit for drinking due to a myriad of potential water-borne diseases. Just being able to drink fresh, clean tap water whenever I wanted was a privilege that I had never been consciously thankful for back home. In Africa, our water bottles not only accompanied us to meals and physical activities, but also to the bathroom, since we had to use bottled water to brush our teeth.

Warm showers and clean, bug-free, indoor bathrooms with Western toilets were something I completely took for granted in my normal life in America. When I returned home from my safari, I often got flashbacks to when my only toilet option consisted of wading through tall grasses, worrying about ticks jumping up my ass, and taking special caution not to ruin my shoes as I squatted above the dirt. I now feel immensely thankful for the simple joy of a Western toilet. It's truly difficult to appreciate what we have until we experience life without the things we consider basic necessities.

Upon my return home, it felt like absolute freedom to abandon my daily routine of taking malaria pills and worrying that I might encounter an unknown illness if I brushed my teeth with unclean tap water. To feel the cold blast of air conditioning on my hot skin was a foreign sensation, one that I relished with a level of joy characteristic of a child tasting ice cream for the first time.

I knew that living the camping lifestyle for nearly two months would challenge me and force me to learn to cope with minimal luxuries, but I had not realized how the experience would fundamentally change my baseline of what is "normal" or a "necessity." After spending so long living with so little, I have a renewed appreciation for the simple pleasures in life—waking up in an actual bed, using a real toilet, and even the innocent joy of flicking on a light switch, rather than donning a headlamp to be able to navigate my living quarters after sunset.

Though the Swahili word "safari" translates to journey, I believe this journey is not exclusively of the African wilderness variety. To live the safari life does not mean you must camp out in the wilderness and come face-to-face with the stars of Animal Planet on a daily basis. Safari life is a mindset of treating every day as a journey. A few weeks of living the safari life gave me a new normal filled with incredible unique experiences that don't happen in everyday life at home. But I'm also thankful for the discomfort that came with that new normal. Enduring the struggles made me gain a new level of gratitude for life's little luxuries that I formerly took for granted.

Zambia and Zimbabwe: Navigating a Coronavirus Detour

"Life is a series of natural and spontaneous changes.
Don't resist them—that only creates sorrow. Let reality be reality.
Let things flow naturally forward in whatever way they like."

—Lao Tzu

Floating on a houseboat in the middle of Lake Kariba in Zimbabwe, there were no roosters to crow a sunrise song. Instead, the melodic morning grunts of hippos served as our wake-up call. I got up and leaned over the railing of the houseboat, peering across the placid waters towards the mountains in the distance to see if I could spot a mother hippo and the miniature versions of herself lurking just below the water's surface.

Just a few hours earlier, in the post-midnight indigo haze, I had been staring at a bright orange supermoon—a moon so bright it could be mistaken for the sun. The supermoon's orange glow peeked above the horizon where the lake met the mountains just as the sun winked its last goodbye on the opposite side of the vast blue expanse of water. The brushstrokes of pinks and yellows that the sun left in its wake adorned the Western half of the sky, while the vibrant orange of the supermoon dominated the East. It was a unique moment, with the sunset overlapping the moonrise, on a unique date, when the serenity of my safari vacation began overlapping with the chaos engulfing the world in early March 2020.

While I was admiring the supermoon in this remote location in the middle of Lake Kariba, where the sounds of the nearest city were hundreds of miles away and an Internet connection was a figment of the imagination, the majority of the world was tuned into something else. Elsewhere around the world, daily news briefings blared out the latest updates about country lockdowns and rising death tolls as the coronavirus pandemic began to pick up steam and wreak havoc across the globe.

For us, the week of coronavirus news unfolded one huge, unexpected announcement at a time. Shocking closures and major event cancellations hit our inboxes whenever we got a chance every other day or so to connect to the Internet and download updates on the latest news.

During that pivotal second week in March, the world had been watching coronavirus unfold across Europe, America, Latin America, and even places as seemingly remote as Australia. The virus was expanding from its original epicenter in Asia and increasing in severity day by day. Most people were glued to their phones or TVs for constant updates those days, bracing themselves for unprecedented college campus closures and cancellations of iconic events and gatherings such as conferences and music festivals that had never before missed a year in history. Surgical-grade N-95 masks, anti-bacterial alcohol-based hand sanitizer, and the concept of "social distancing" were the new phrases on everyone's lips.

While the rest of the world was drinking from a firehose and suffering from COVID-19 information overload, our news source was like a broken faucet, only spilling out a few drops of vital information every now and then.

First, we found out the Nepal government had closed down Mount Everest for the entire 2020 climbing season. This was the first major wrench in my plans, since a Mount Everest base camp trek had been on deck for Maddy and I a few short weeks after our African safari was scheduled to wrap up. Then, we received news that our friends back at our home universities, New York University and Princeton, had to evacuate campus and resort to online classes for at least the next month. We thanked our past selves for somehow having the most opportune foresight: I had chosen to graduate a semester early and Maddy had been in the middle of a gap year, so we would never have the unfortunate experience of attending "Zoom university" as many of our peers did.

The previous week, before arriving at the houseboat, we had stopped at a hospital in rural Malawi while touring a village. Meeting with the doctor and understanding more about the challenges of running a clinic in a rural area made me realize how I always assumed that if I were to get sick, my country's healthcare system would be there to save me. This hospital visit made it painfully evident that healthcare infrastructure in many areas of rural Africa could not possibly handle a pandemic sending significant percentages of the population into emergency rooms. If multiple people became sick and needed hospital beds, proper personal protective equipment such as masks and gloves, and plexiglass panels between beds to prevent patients from coughing and contaminating one another, were lacking. The hospital we visited made the situation seem bleak and nearly impossible to deal with, considering the extremely contagious and unknown nature of COVID-19.

A few days after that hospital visit, we stopped at a grocery store to restock our food for the next few days of camping. Next to the cash register, a local newsletter headline exclaimed in ominous, bold letters: CORONAVIRUS SUSPECT ESCAPED. The fanaticism surrounding this unfamiliar disease—using the word "suspect" as if it were someone convicted of a crime—conveyed itself in the boldness of the headline. Reading deeper, I gleaned that someone who had flown into Zimbabwe from Thailand, and who was potentially carrying the virus, had fled from the hospital before they could quarantine him. At the time, merely one potential suspected case of COVID-19 in the entire country of Zimbabwe felt like a significant threat.

Despite being in nearly the middle of nowhere, the coronavirus was finding its way toward me and my travel plans, slowly, but surely.

Fast forward a few days after disembarking from the houseboat, the sound of my flip flops smacking against my feet reverberated through the air. I was running down a dirt road, kicking up red-brown sediment onto the backs of my legs. My arms were contorted at odd angles from clutching rolls of toilet paper, hand sanitizer, and soap tightly against my chest, trying to prevent anything from falling onto the dirt path that led me back to my hostel in Victoria Falls, Zimbabwe.

Dozens of worrisome thoughts bounced around in my head just like the rolls of toilet paper bouncing around in my arms: *I can't believe there's toilet paper shortages in the United States right now! What's going to happen to me if I get stopped at the airport and can't catch my flight before the South African border closes? Where is the nearest place I could possibly find a face mask in the middle of Zimbabwe? Who ever thought that this novel coronavirus was going to get this bad?*

It was now mid-March 2020, a time that nearly every person on this planet who lived through the coronavirus pandemic probably remembers as the global turning point. Italy was under lockdown, the US was encouraging citizens abroad to come home as soon as possible, airlines were abruptly suspending service to and from COVID-19 hot spots, and countries throughout Africa were closing their borders left and right on short notice. Reaching the end of my seven-week safari was starting to look as impossible as finding an N-95 mask in the middle of an overland camping trip.

Six weeks earlier, when my flight touched down in Kenya, I would have been confused if you told me my last prominent memory of this African overland camping safari adventure would be running down the street, clutching various household cleaning and disinfectant products.

I had tried, at first, to believe that I would be safer if I just stayed the course and proceeded on my journey as originally intended. In the early days of that pivotal week, Africa was starting to seem like the ideal place to be—no lockdown in sight. Maddy and I initially joked about how we were safer staying in Africa than returning to the populous New York City metro area, where the risk of contracting the virus seemed to be much higher in terms of population density and COVID-19 case count at the time. There were significantly more cases in New York City than there were in even the entire continent of Africa, at that point in time. But just a few short days later, border closures and the thought of getting stranded in Zimbabwe or Botswana drove home the seriousness of the situation: lack of adequate health insurance, stable hospital infrastructure, or even a long-term place to stay in case of a lockdown order made going home the rational option.

Reality hit us—we could not escape the path of this virus. I crouched around my phone to take advantage of the free Wi-Fi, as I relentlessly refreshed the page. The words I had been dreading suddenly flashed across the screen during the president of South Africa's COVID-19 update briefing: "The South African government will enact border closures in the next 48 hours. All inbound flights will cease."

These words sent me into a scramble. Since South Africa was the most developed country in the southern region of the African continent, we had been told that other countries such as Botswana—our intended next destination—would follow suit and close their borders, rather than wait until the case count in the country was out of control.

I immediately exited the South African government webpage and pulled up a Google Flights query for last-minute flights home. In order to get from my current location in Zimbabwe to New York City, I needed to get a connecting flight through South Africa. If the borders were closing in 48 hours, I basically needed to be on a flight tomorrow to be sure that I could get out of the country and home in time without running into potential complications.

This frantic, last-minute ticket search cost me over $3000 for a single one-way flight in economy class. Clearly, there was enormous demand from fellow travelers who found themselves in southern Africa at this worst possible time. I had once been the type of person who would have said, "Travel insurance is just a way for companies to make money off of your fear!" but now I could not stop thanking myself for buying travel insurance for the first time ever. My African safari required travel insurance to cover potential injuries and trip interruptions such as this emergency flight home.

Once the flight was booked, I didn't even have time to relax as I started counting down the hours until I would start the long, worrisome journey home.

Airports were supposedly the most dangerous locations, with so many people coming from different countries and mingling in an epicenter of tightly-packed waiting lines and enclosed spaces—the exact opposite of where leading epidemiologists would recommend someone to be at a time like this.

In addition to the stress and sadness, I was in a state of disbelief. From the few texts and news updates that trickled through my spotty Internet connection, I developed the understanding that my family and friends were running into serious trouble not being able to find toilet paper, hand sanitizer, or soap. News reports had sensationalized the concept of shelter-in-place for an indefinite period of time, and Americans had taken these warnings to the extreme by hoarding essential supplies, causing many stores to turn customers away when sanitary essentials were out of stock.

I had felt like a hero running down that dirt road with the valuable goods in hand. Never before had I felt so victorious for just buying simple household items such as toilet paper and soap.

With these COVID-19 survival essentials stocked in my backpack, I turned to the group of fellow travelers I had spent the past six weeks with on this camping safari. All of us were grappling with how our big, ambitious travel plans were toppling down like a poorly assembled tent back from our first week of camping. I happened to be the first of our group to secure a flight home, and sadly, made the rounds, exchanging tear-filled goodbyes and best wishes for the inevitably complicated journeys home. We all hugged each other tightly, as if clinging to each other could help us hold on to the past six weeks of laughter around the campfire, shenanigans on safari vehicles, and once-in-a-lifetime wildlife encounters that we would only ever be able to reminisce about with each other. Little did I know at the time that these goodbye hugs would be the last time I would hug someone who didn't live in my household for nearly a year.

When it came down to the last person to say goodbye to—my travel buddy, Maddy—the past few weeks on this overland safari flashed before my eyes: Maddy's face covered in the brown dust of the Serengeti after sticking our heads out of the roofs of the safari vehicles; the look of pure terror in her eyes when a cheetah jumped on the hood of our truck; the beaming grin lighting up her face as we watched baby elephants awkwardly stumble through tall grasses. We couldn't stop each other from weeping, as she cried out in a choked voice, "I don't wanna go home!"

For Maddy and I, half of our tears stemmed from reflecting on the past six weeks spending every second of the day together on our African safari adventure, coming face-to-face with animals and situations that we had never before dreamed of encountering. The other half of our tears were prompted by the thought of the remainder of the trip that we were cancelling and forgoing by heading home—the beaches of Sri Lanka; the snow-covered passes of the Himalayas; and the street food of Singapore, which is where we had first met each other. We never imagined this journey around the world to end by parting ways early and going home to simply sit in our houses and quarantine. After the round of goodbyes, my eyes were watery the entire way from the hostel to the airport, where I would begin the long journey home.

I caught my first flight from Victoria Falls, Zimbabwe to the international airport in Johannesburg, South Africa. Knowing so many flights from different countries with varying degrees of COVID-19 severity criss-crossed and deposited passengers in this South African airport hub, it felt like a war zone, where the enemy could be behind any corner. The fear was palpable, as everyone seemed to move in slow motion out of caution, trying to keep their distance and touch as few surfaces as possible.

Worry and uncertainty seemed to wrap around everyone like a blanket. It was almost suffocating going through the airport security lines, having to get close to one another and fearing that anyone might have this virus that could endanger our lives and the lives of our families back home.

One woman in line ahead of me turned around with a wide-eyed look of shock and apprehension as she waved her hands around her face and gestured at the air, saying, "It lives here, not here!" pointing down at the objects on the security conveyor belt. In any other situation, I might have thought she was crazy and talking about ghosts or some supernatural being, not an invisible airborne virus.

During the waiting period at the airport before my flight, I washed my hands with proper soap and water more times in just a few hours than I had in the past six weeks, when running water had been largely unavailable on our extended camping trip. Every single time I sat down in the airport and touched even just the handle of a chair or the bottom of my own backpack, I instinctively made a beeline toward the restroom to vigorously scrub my hands, just in case. With no face masks available in the airport, I pulled a scarf over my face and tried as much as possible to breathe only my own air, stay back from other people, and not let anyone touch my bags.

Once aboard the flight and settled into my seat, I was about to let my thoughts drift off but was interrupted from doing so when someone waved and caught my attention.

"Ma'am, is this bag in the overhead bin yours? Could you please move it? I don't want to, you know, touch it... but I need to make some space for my own bag."

It felt like an alternate universe to think about how in a normal situation, it would be no problem at all for someone to shove aside my baggage in the overhead bin, but now, it was socially necessary to ask me to touch my own bag, as we all knew to refrain from putting our hands and potential germs on anything that wasn't ours. Rather than spending the entire flight consciously worrying about who was breathing on me or potentially infecting me, I allowed my brain to power off as I slept for the entire 15-hour flight home.

When I touched down in New York at the John F. Kennedy Airport and there was no COVID-19 screening procedure in place, I stared back at the customs and border patrol agent in disbelief. She had merely asked me if my flight had originated from Italy or China, as if those were the only two places in the world where coronavirus existed. Everyone was walking through the security gates into the outside world, ready to mingle with millions of other New Yorkers, without even so much as a temperature scan to check for active symptoms of the virus.

Many people consider Africa to be a "primitive" continent, lacking the technology and development of Western countries like America, but this stereotype did not hold true in certain key aspects during the time of COVID-19. Throughout my entire six weeks traveling through Kenya, Tanzania, Zanzibar, Malawi, Zambia, and Zimbabwe, nearly every border we crossed had a border patrol guard on hand to administer a temperature check. The irony was that these temperature checks were initially in place from the Ebola pandemic that happened only a few years ago, making this so-called "undeveloped" continent truly more well-equipped than a country like America that considers itself to be the shining example of the most developed nation in the world.

Despite these technological differences, it was striking to think about how difficult it would be for many villages in Africa to survive the pandemic. As I reached my home destination, I reflected about how I was fortunate enough to be able to quarantine in a household fully stocked with supplies and ample room to move around indoors.

I felt deep empathy for the typical family in many of the rural villages that I had passed through on my travels. A local guide had grimly explained to me, the concept of social distancing is nearly impossible where people live in close quarters and where there's no such thing as grocery or food delivery services to eliminate the need to leave your home. Access to a mask or gloves or hand sanitizer is a rare privilege. Most strikingly, the guide remarked, "How are we supposed to convince these local people that they need to buy soap, when they can barely afford food? You can't expect people to prioritize addressing larger, more ambiguous issues like this new virus when they can't even fulfill their basic needs and put food on the table."

Thinking back about the kind local guides and families I interacted with during my trip throughout southeastern Africa, I fear that I have experienced a version of these African countries that will no longer exist in the same form after the pandemic. Tourism is a symbiotic relationship. We travelers may treat visiting a new country as a vacation or an opportunity to explore new perspectives, and sometimes may forget that we are also supporting the dreams and livelihoods of local entrepreneurs whose families depend on income from tourists. I hope that these hard-working entrepreneurs are able to find a way to survive this unprecedented pause in global tourism that struck the world beginning in 2020.

Although the COVID-19 pandemic put a stop to my global travel plans and felt like the end of the world to me at the time, thinking about the people I met in Africa helped put in perspective that if my worst concern about the pandemic was a trip being canceled, I was among the lucky few.

USA: Rediscovering America and Myself

*"Why do you go away? So that you can come back.
So that you can see the place you came from
with new eyes and extra colors... Coming back
to where you started is not the same as never leaving."*

—Terry Pratchett

"You girls are at a Trump rally; you know that, right? Trump announced a surprise rally here in Maine after his visit to New Hampshire last night."

I blankly stared back at the woman dressed in camo clothing as my mind raced with confusion. Suddenly, the Make America Great Again hats glowing red in the back of pickup trucks and the Trump 2020 bumper stickers that we saw on our way to this farm all clicked into place.

On a random Saturday in October 2020, my friends and I, who, at the time, were living and working remotely in a temporary home for a month near Acadia National Park on the coast of Maine, had decided to drive a few hours inland for some wholesome fun at a corn maze at Treworgy Family Orchards.

But we ended up experiencing more than just a typical day in rural Maine. We unintentionally found ourselves in the presence of then President Donald Trump himself. It was just weeks before the contentious election where Biden and Trump would go head-to-head to determine the fate of the not-so-United States of America.

Although my friends and I were far from being Trump supporters, we decided to stay at the farm since we had already made the
drive. It also felt a bit like fate was telling us we were supposed
to have this potentially empathy-building experience. After all,
what were the odds that at the exact time, on the exact date that
we randomly decided to seek out a corn maze for fun, the president of the United States would select that exact same time and
place to make a surprise, previously unscheduled visit?

Feeling like undercover spies, and sticking out uncomfortably as
apparently the only non-whites in the entire crowd of thousands
of Maine residents, we shuffled into the long line of people decked
out in Trump shirts, hats, jackets, phone cases, and even capes. Despite being in the midst of a global pandemic where cities across
the world were once again experiencing spikes of coronavirus
hospitalizations, not a single face mask was in sight at this gath-
ering of thousands of people. America, at that time, was a place
where scientific facts could somehow be misconstrued as political opinions.

Our comfort zone of the liberally-minded melting pot of New
York City felt like it was light years away. But still we stayed, seek-
ing to perhaps better understand what we felt was an enigma in
American identity.

The whir of the presidential helicopter transporting Donald
Trump himself over the cornfields of rural Maine drowned out the
whoops and cheers of the fanatical supporters in front and behind
us. The mob of people waiting to get checked by the Secret Service
before being permitted to enter the rally buzzed with excitement.

Moments later, a woman ran through the crowd waving her phone
in the air, proudly showing off her video of standing so close to
President Trump that she could almost touch him. This level of

fanaticism drew me back to middle school days when friends of mine would stalk celebrities like Harry Styles in New York City and cry at the mere sight of their idol.

"Maybe if we speed over to the airport right now, we can catch a final glimpse of him before he leaves our state!" exclaimed one middle-aged man in a bright red Trump 2020 shirt.

Never before had I seen such utter fandom for a president, let alone one who had undoubtedly been the most controversial in recent history. On the complete flip side, my perspective had aligned with entire streets of New York City lined with protestors and those mourning the impending loss of their rights as immigrants, Muslims, and members of the LGBTQ community right after Trump had been elected back in 2016.

Staying in my New York City bubble would have made it easy to assume that most Americans are just like me, in keeping with my own thinking and political beliefs. But moving myself far from my comfort zone to experience life in a new corner of my own country, and ending up at a Trump rally in rural Maine, was an unexpected, yet enlightening, look at the two starkly disparate sides of this country that we call the "United" States of America.

I spent the tail end of 2020 and all of 2021 living the digital nomad life, hopping around the US. I was eager to experience different cities and regions of the country, while working remotely and trying to make the most of life, despite the global pandemic limiting international travels. Through this domestic nomadic journey, I gained the perspectives of many unique communities across the country that make up the micro-cultures and micro-climates of this gigantic nation. Somehow, this nation simultaneously holds the most power and the most potentially conflict-arousing diversity in the world.

Before 2020, I thought that traveling in my own country was boring.

I traveled to understand new cultures, try unique foods, and experience different ways of life. "Why visit Seattle, Denver, or New Orleans when I could, for a similar cost, visit France, Thailand, or Mexico?" thought my naive self. "What could I possibly learn from meeting other Americans?"

In the years leading up to college, and even during college itself, this line of thinking caused me to set my sights on international flights to exotic locations with language barriers.

I remember being disappointed the first time my parents took me to visit the Grand Canyon. Despite being a natural wonder that visitors from all around the world flock to, I complained that this "waste" of time had the opportunity cost of not experiencing a new country and its unique culture somewhere else in the world.

In my mind, to travel domestically was to not truly travel. I developed an aversion to National Parks within the US. Likewise, I considered most American cities to be "too close to home" to be considered "real traveling."

But then 2020 came along and brought with it both the first global pandemic of our lifetimes, and an end to seamless international travel due to flight bans, country border closings, and stay-at-home orders.

Instead of seeing all seven continents in seven months as part of the massive post-grad trip I had spent years dreaming about and planning for, I spent the majority of the year living at my childhood home, barely ever straying a few miles.

With so much free time to think during the early, seemingly endless lockdown days of the pandemic, I started mulling over what it meant to be American. Did I truly know and embody the American identity? Or did I merely know what it meant to grow up specifically in northern New Jersey, and to live in the liberal bubble of a college like New York University? How could any one person identify and represent "America" when it was a place defined by its melting-pot amalgamation of so many diverse, sometimes contrasting, cultures and viewpoints?

I reflected on how fellow travelers and exchange students had reacted to me introducing myself as American over the past few years of my travels abroad. Often saying I was from New York City was somehow less embarrassing than saying I was from America—a word that carried so much potential baggage, with various stereotypes and critical associations influenced by global media coverage and America's often controversial actions on the world stage.

When traveling abroad, I was often the only American in the room. Many times, I was the first American someone had ever met. These encounters taught me firsthand what it meant to be an ambassador and a representative of my culture.

I became someone's window into America, but more specifically, a window into what it's like to be a Filipino-Polish-American who grew up in a predominantly white suburb of a major metropolitan area. I came to realize that it was crucial to qualify my experiences and perspectives with a reminder that the United States was a huge landmass with drastically different environments, both physical and political, in different corners of the nation.

When exchange students from all around Europe, Asia, and Australia asked me what it's like to live in a nation that allows people to carry guns, I was careful to explain the differences in gun laws between different states. I tried not to confirm or deny any American stereotypes ascribed to my nationality, and that weren't necessarily my lived experience.

The first time I had to explain to a non-American the concept of doing an active shooter drill, in addition to a fire drill at school, was when I realized how entirely foreign my country must seem. Their home country, devoid of the right to bear arms as dictated in our centuries-old Constitution, operated under completely different circumstances, without the real potential of spontaneous shootings when merely going to school, or the grocery store, or a movie theater. America was a place like no other, for better or for worse.

The more I thought about my experience introducing myself to others abroad and explaining the metropolitan East Coast experience, the more I realized that visiting a different part of your home state or home country can bring valuable different perspectives and learnings just as much as seeing a new country.

During my time as a domestic nomad, I learned a little bit more about myself and the Americans who call different corners of the country home.

After spending a month living outside Acadia National Park in a cabin in Maine, nestled in between deciduous trees whose leaves burned bright orange and yellow, I nurtured a previously underdeveloped appreciation for nature. I learned that outside the business-oriented financial and creative hub of New York City that I had always known, entire industries like lobster fishing, with their own culture and nuances, supported a majority of the economy of states like Maine.

I witnessed, unfortunately, how lack of ethnic diversity could cause a waitress in Maine to remark, "You speak English so well!" out of ignorance, rather than malice, to my two Chinese friends who were, in fact, born in America. Being surrounded by nature can be rejuvenating and awe-inspiring, but also often comes at the cost of being away from cultural epicenters that enrich our ability to understand and connect with others from different backgrounds.

Two months of living within walking distance of Pacific Beach in San Diego meant post-work strolls to see the sunset over the ocean; 99-cent beachside fish tacos; weekend camping trips in the desert; and boardwalk roller skating sessions. But most importantly, it also meant two months of embracing a West Coast mentality after a brutal, strictly-indoors COVID winter on the East Coast.

My mental health had been at an all-time low when I first reached San Diego in early January 2021. The serenity of the ocean and the ability to spend time outdoors in the depths of winter—something near impossible in the Northeast where I had always lived—gave me the mental stability to persevere through tough times. I learned how to prioritize my mental health, rather than always adding new things to my plate in the over-ambitious style of a New Yorker.

A three-month stint in San Francisco taught me the gradual process of creating a sense of home and showed me, firsthand, how a city and environment shapes you as a person. During my college years in New York City, my weekends had been filled with expensive boozy brunches; strutting down Fifth Avenue in business clothes; strolling through Central Park with a $7-latte in hand; and embracing the fast-paced, glamorous aura of the city.

Meanwhile, San Francisco taught me that there's more to a city than brunch and nightlife. The Bay Area's temperate but breezy weather made it easy to dress for comfort, rather than style. Though there was a large presence of tech industry professionals, their laid-back mentality contrasted the high-strung energy of 100-hour-work-week bankers and consultants in New York City.

My conversations with new friends in San Francisco centered around sustainability and best hikes within driving distance. The mentality and preferences of my social circle in San Francisco differed dramatically from that of my friends in New York City. I realized that I had been contorting myself to fit the mold of a New Yorker for years, even though I truly was not a fan of nightlife and concrete jungles devoid of hiking and escapes into nature.

Though New York City will always feel like home since I spent my college years there, San Francisco showed me that home is more than a single location. Home is a feeling that you are finally in a place that fits your life without you having to change who you are to fit the vibe of that location. Home is not necessarily your hometown, but is wherever you feel like you belong.

I will forever be thankful that I chose to reject stability and challenge myself outside of my comfort zone by moving to Maine, then San Diego, then San Francisco, then Los Angeles for no reason other than wanting to test out the waters of a new city.

After nearly half a year of gallivanting around the country, I had made plans to sublet an apartment and spend my summer in New York City, so I could take a break from exploring and simply enjoy the familiarity of my established social circles and old haunts.

But life said "psych!" and continued to challenge me to reject my comfort zone. Only about a week before I was supposed to move back to New York, I was invited to move into a Beverly Hills mansion that used to belong to Paris Hilton. There, I would spend a month living with startup founders and content creators, while spending time finalizing this book and taking steps toward launching other travel-related entrepreneurial ventures that aligned with my true passions.

With the glamor of Hollywood and so many industries centered around vanity and self-promotion, I never imagined myself living in or liking Los Angeles. But just like San Francisco, the city of angels exceeded my expectations and challenged my assumptions by providing me one of the most valuable, enjoyable, and pivotal months of my life. Much like San Francisco felt like home when I was searching for others who shared an appreciation for nature and a distaste for blowing money in New York City, Los Angeles felt like home when I was considering quitting my full-time job at Instagram to work full-time on making a living off travel writing and content creation.

I became intoxicated and hooked on the creative energy of Los Angeles, fueled by meeting hundreds of self-employed entrepreneurs and creators. Knowing others were working tirelessly to map their own unique career paths gave me the confidence to chart my own course, as well. After just two weeks in Los Angeles, I submitted my two weeks' notice and quit my job to travel full-time. Living amidst other creators helped me realize I wanted to spend my time and energy creating a community of travelers who, like me, could learn and grow from their experiences around the world.

Despite my original perception that domestic travel could never teach me anything, living in various corners of the United States allowed me to embrace different mentalities and valuable lessons about myself and my values. If I had stayed in my hometown, rather than voluntarily choosing to explore new places, I would not have had the perspective-shifting experiences that shaped my personal and professional path into what it is today. Through re-discovering America, I rediscovered myself.

Epilogue: The Journey Continues

"And then there is the most dangerous risk of all—
the risk of spending your life not doing what you want
on the bet you can buy yourself the freedom to do it later."

—Randy Komisar

There's no cure for curiosity. You can see more places and it will just leave you wanting more, rather than making you feel satisfied to give up the pursuit.

The day that I abandoned my African safari due to the onset of a global pandemic was, ironically, exactly three years after that fateful day I woke up on the floor of a mud hut in Ghana and promised myself to prioritize travel and find a way to visit all seven continents during college. Life has an uncanny way of making significant events align.

Three years, seventy countries, and seven continents later, I can happily look back at my 18-year-old self's ambitions knowing that "travel more" definitely became the mantra that defined my formative young adult years. As documented through the stories and reflections that comprise this book, I've explored the world while also exploring the deeper layers of myself. Capping off these three travel-intensive years with a pandemic-induced travel ban is something I never would have anticipated nor hoped for.

But in an optimistic view, the coronavirus age of cancelled plans made me realize that sometimes we might not get exactly what we want, but the universe finds a way to give us what we need.

In the early days of the pandemic lockdown, I spent so much time just being upset about the state of the world. However, when it became obvious that shelter-in-place wasn't going to end anytime soon, I realized that I had to make the most of things. Although I never would've intentionally wanted to be stuck at home for months on end, an opportunity to reflect and recharge was actually exactly what I needed.

Without extended downtime during lockdown and the pause on international travel, this book would likely not exist. My go-go-go lifestyle of maximizing every weekend abroad and jetting across the world on every break or holiday never would have permitted the quiet reflection that brought forth these stories about my unique travel experiences and moments of realization that no one else could have written but me.

As much as I miss traveling and do wish I had been able to complete my originally planned seven-continents-in-seven-months journey around the world, I believe that everything happens for a reason. I'm grateful for the opportunity that life presented me to switch gears and refocus during 2020.

Writing this book served as a conduit for reflecting on what I've learned through traveling. It's been an arduous process to analyze my own memories and tease out the meaningful experiences that have left an impact. But it's been rewarding to focus on creating this time capsule that brings both personal satisfaction, and hopefully, reader inspiration. The thought of having this artifact of my 22-year-old self to look back on, and even to read to my kids and grandkids one day, has motivated me to work hard and complete this book. I treasure this opportunity to document how travel has shaped my personality and worldview.

All these lessons from traveling have made me who I am today. Adjusting my pace of life to fit my environment, proactively seeking a taste of new cultures, learning to empathize with previously foreign lived experiences, embracing a duty to conserve the earth, not allowing expectations to distort my perception of reality, understanding my own racial identity, appreciating the simple things I formerly took for granted, learning to confront my ignorance head-on, and making the most out of unexpected situations are key life skills acquired firsthand through travel.

Whenever I feel like a problem is insurmountable, I can recall scaling mountains and surviving life-threatening situations, putting things back in perspective. Having been through unfamiliar situations abroad where I was the furthest possible distance from my comfort zone, I know that my obstacles back home pale in comparison.

Living out of a backpack for months at a time taught me it's fully possible to get by with minimal material possessions. Since I've previously adjusted to the simple life on the road, I hardly complain or yearn for luxury because I know I can survive with less. Most importantly, I can be happy with less.

My nomadic existence during college gave me a glimpse of so many different ways of life. I now get to create my own.

A well-traveled life is full of inspiration, but it also creates a paradox of choice. I've met strikingly different people who each have found happiness and fulfillment in their own ways. I've walked through hundreds of cities that each offer a unique feeling of "home." Collecting all these diverse perspectives is merely the first step. I am now faced with the challenge of synthesizing these learnings to better inform my life decisions.

My concept of how to live a good life was initially formed by the limited perspectives and reference points of a sheltered upbringing in my suburban hometown. Post-travel, I now know that my way of living is not the only way to live. Repeatedly faced with discomfort and strangeness in foreign lands, I grew to question my opinions and values and have adopted new ways of seeing the world.

By repeatedly physically displacing myself, I've been able to identify which of my beliefs were a product of my cultural upbringing. These location-specific or culture-specific beliefs are easy to identify because they are often the source of discomfort when exploring a new country. Shedding your initial culture-specific beliefs gives space for new beliefs and perspectives from a foreign culture to squeeze themselves into your core values during your travels.

The values I held that did not shift in different cultural contexts are the beliefs that are fundamental to who I am. By separating my fundamental values from my societally-imposed values, I've grown more conscious and intentional about what I believe, why I believe it, and where the source of that belief stems from.

When I think about what's next for myself, I don't yet know if a future of constant location change is the long-term life I want to lead. A travel-curious mind creates a sustained restlessness that isn't easily satisfied. But, investing time to deeply immerse in one place, even if just exploring new areas within my own home country, can also be extremely rewarding. I still firmly believe that you are where you go, but that doesn't necessarily mean you need to be going to different places all the time.

Though sifting through the likes and dislikes of my past experiences and aligning myself with one particular place or lifestyle seems daunting, I find comfort in the fact that my decisions moving forward in life will be well-informed, thanks to the perspectives I've collected from all different corners of the world.

Many people grow up hearing the phrase, "You are what you eat" as a guiding principle to convey that consuming nutritious, hearty food will make you a good, healthy person. We can control what we put into our bodies, so this guidance makes perfect sense.

But what if someone told you from a young age that "You are where you go"? Would you shift your priorities to visit as many diverse, interesting, and unique places as possible in order to fulfill the identity you aspire for? Are the places you've been an accurate portrayal of the values and interests you hold within you? Would you be more intentional about playing the role of an active observer, taking in everything that a new place has to offer, rather than merely a passenger on a trip with sites and experiences whizzing by but not being absorbed?

If you gain only one thing from reading this book, I hope that it's the realization that travel is more than an opportunity to enhance your Instagram profile or to get drunk on a beach surrounded by people speaking a foreign tongue. Travel is a tool for self-development. Exploration can be life's greatest teacher, if you let it be.

Travel soon. Travel often. Travel with an open mind and a malleable set of values. Put yourself in unfamiliar situations, make mistakes, and learn from them sooner rather than later. Enduring the hardships of travel only makes you stronger. Much like diamonds, we all need a little pressure before we can become fully formed.

Travel because you can collect experiences. Travel because no one can ever take away your memories; no natural disaster can ever destroy the moments that you've enjoyed. Purchases and possessions may come into and out of your life, but travel is one accomplishment that no one can value as much as you do for yourself. See as much of the world for yourself as you can.

No two people have the exact same trip to Florence, or the exact same animal sightings on a safari, or the exact same route and emotional experience when trekking through Patagonia. You and your own perspectives, with your own perception of "normal" from wherever you come from and whatever you've been exposed to, make your travel experiences unique.

Beauty is truly in the eye of the beholder, and so too is the concept of "normal." What is normal in one corner of the world may be anything but normal on the opposite side of the world. Each new perspective you gain changes your understanding of what is "weird" and what is "normal," until one day you realize that to define something as normal is to designate other things as abnormal. Evolving to understand the world beyond categorizations of "normal" is one of the first steps to understanding that one culture's way of doing things is neither right nor wrong—just different.

Exploring a new place may often be seen as an escape from the everyday, but it is never an escape from yourself. Physically, you are where you go. Mentally, you become where you have been. A change of scenery forces you to confront change, but also forces you to reconcile that people come and go, and you can shift location, but you and your identity are the constants in your own life. Absorbing variables from diverse environments in the form of lessons and perspectives is the best way to strengthen your own concept of self.

My jaunts in unfamiliar locales forced me to figure out myself and focus on learning from my environment and experiences as much as I can because no matter where I go, I will always be myself. I am where I've been. Newfound philosophies and habits picked up on the road have led me to a richer life in which I am more sure of my values, which ultimately translates into happiness. You are where you go. So where will you go next?

"Travel far enough, you meet yourself."

—David Mitchell

Acknowledgments

To finally hold this book in my hands and to see my life's most meaningful stories and character-defining moments forever memorialized is nothing short of a dream come true.

Although there is only my name on the cover of this book, an entire village of collaborators and supporters played a key role in transforming my key life experiences into the book you're reading.

This is where, if I could, I would fill hundreds and hundreds of pages with the simple yet powerful words: "thank you." This book would not exist if I were on this journey alone.

To my mom and dad—thank you for the endless support. Dad, thank you for always being the first person to read and provide feedback for each of my chapters as I progressed one-by-one during the creation of my first draft manuscript. Thank you both for providing endless hugs and encouragement whenever I doubted myself during this creative writing process. When I decided I wanted to quit my prestigious, stable full time job at Instagram to pursue my passions, thank you both for supporting me and believing in my ability to create the life that I want for myself.

To my sister, Ashley—thank you for being my instant-feedback sounding board and sidekick throughout life. I hope that you, too, can explore the world, explore yourself, and discover that you are where you go.

To Amy, my fellow author and number one supporter through it all—this book exists thanks to you and your encouragement to take the leap of faith, invest the time, and capture my thoughts and stories in print. You are my rock and my number one fan, and I'm so proud to call you my best friend.

To Michael, the unofficial creative director of my life and a true friend—without your creative juices and our immensely helpful brainstorm sessions, this book would look quite different. Thank you for taking the time to give me thoughtful feedback at every stage of my book creation process over the past year, from my initial title brainstorming to cover concepts to chapter titles and everything in between.

To Adam—thank you for being my partner in travel and in life. It was this book that sparked our first conversation about traveling together, which transitioned into countless actual trips together. Your unwavering support, confidence in my abilities, and emphatic encouragement always make me feel like anything, including writing and publishing this book, is possible.

To Simmi, Shreya, Krithika, Ruchi, and Sahitya—your support and excitement about my writing and creative journey has kept me going for months, especially during the toughest times when I was so close to giving up. For all the love, positivity, and good vibes, I am so thankful.

To Maddie and Andrew—thank you for supporting me from the very beginning through the very end. From reading drafts of my initial chapters to listening to all my various podcasts where I talk about my book and my travels, your support and excitement makes me feel so loved and appreciated by amazing friends like you.

To my teachers and professors—thank you for opening my mind and enabling me to be a life-long learner. My academic journey in the classroom formed the solid foundation of knowledge that I build upon each and every day as the world around me teaches me new lessons. I treasure the support and encouragement of every educator who has encouraged me and improved my writing and critical thinking skills over the years.

To my study abroad advisors—thank you for working with me to accomplish perhaps the most global academic experience possible within three and a half years of college. Your love of travel and the power of learning through experiencing life abroad is infectious and I am so thankful you empowered me to embark on this journey!

To Hannah and Sebastian— thank you for both indulging me with hour-long conversations about your motivations for study abroad and what travel means to you.

To Eric Koester and all the author coaches at the Creator Institute—thank you for giving me the tools, mindsets, and structure to shape my ideas and verbal stories into an actual 25,000 word first draft manuscript. Without the guidance and accountability of this program, I'm fairly sure this book would have been put on hold for years.

To Diedre—thank you for your developmental editing that helped me transition from a fresh college grad accustomed to academic writing into a writer who understands the importance of dialogue, scenery description, and the nuances of authentic travel writing.

To Maria—thank you for copyediting my entire manuscript and ensuring that my stories had the utmost clarity and authenticity.

To Colby, Kristin, and the entire Palmetto Publishing team—thank you for bringing my cover design concept to life, for allowing the flexibility I desired for my publication timeline, and for being supportive along this entire journey.

To Priyanka Surio, Tiffany Mosher, and Kathiana LeJeune, my fellow travel authors—thank you for providing advice and encouragement during my early stages and for supporting me throughout my book launch! Your commitment to telling your own stories and promoting authentic, character-shaping travel experiences inspires me.

To Alice, Maddy, Nicole, and Iva—thank you for supporting me through my toughest times when I debated entirely giving up on this book. I treasure our memories as roommates in San Diego and San Francisco deeply!

To Alex—thank you for encouraging me and inspiring me endlessly with your passion for helping others. You truly embody what it means to be resilient and optimistic and I am so lucky to have met you!

To everyone who attended my book presale launch party in Los Angeles—thank you!! It is one of the most prized memories of my life seeing so many friends and supporters in one room, especially knowing that I have such true friends who traveled so far to be there and support me on a pivotal day in my author journey.

To Mauro, Makena, Lilly, Elliot, Neyl, Cydne, Alice, Marco, Chloe, Peggy, Andrew, Maddy, and Shannon—thank you for taking the time to read my early chapters before they were released to the world! Your thoughtful feedback helped boost my confidence and shape these stories into the best they could be.

To my *You Are Where You Go* beta reader community—thank you for believing me and supporting me before the book was even released! Your support during my presale campaign not only made this book financially possible, but made me feel more loved and appreciated than I had ever felt before in my life.

To the friends I traveled with throughout the years—thank you for living these moments with me. I hope you've enjoyed reading my side of these travel stories!

To the Launch House community—thank you for supporting my vision and giving me the confidence to quit my corporate job and pursue my passions in the realm of travel. This community singlehandedly accelerated my commitment to pursuing travel-related entrepreneurship and has given me the foundation to be a knowledgeable and connected creator and founder of my own unique career path.

To all the friends who hosted me on their couches during my summer 2021 nomadic journey across the US—thank you for providing a safe haven of productivity and caffeination as this book's creation journey became as nomadic as my own life. I wrote the final chapters and put the finishing touches on this book during a time when I spent each week in a different city... what else would you expect from me at this point? :)

And to you, dear reader—thank you for picking up this book and reading it to completion. I hope that my stories have been able to spark the travel bug within you and stoke your curiosity about the world. I am excited for you to discover for yourself that you are where you go!

For preordering and providing early support, I'll always be thankful to:

Aaron Siegal-Eisman · Abhinav Agarwal · Adam Hussain · Aidan Wolf · AJ Subudhi · Ajay Jain · Albert Tian · Alden Lebov · Alec Reimon · Alexandra Nguyen · Alice Berlin · Alice Wistar · Alix Barasch · Alston Lin · Amanda Brastad · Amanda He · Aminata Diallo · Amrutha Yarlagadda · Amy Dong · Ana Martinez · Andon Parascando · Andres Gomez Perry · Andrew Giles · Andrew Han · Andy Nguyen · Angela Huang · Antonio DiMeglio · Aren Melkonian · Ariella Reuben · Armina Hall · Ashley Irick · Ashley Lubas · Austin Gregory · Avagail Lozano · Awele Asianah · Ayotomiwa Akinyele · Belinda Li · Brandy Chen · Brendan Ngo · Brian Hanssen · Caitlin Ner · Carolin Carella · Carolina Diaz · Cat Li · Chelsea Mortell · Cherie McLaughlin · Chris Pacitto · Christian Blanchet · Christine Nguyen · Christopher Klann · Conrad DeMasi · Crystal Lillard · Cydne Dufort · Dan Keyser · Dana Zhang · Daniel Neckonoff · Dannika Thompson · Denalia Zhi · Dimitris Kalimeris · Eeshaan Rao · Elisa Zhang · Elizabeth Petisme-Alip · Elizabeth Serviss · Emily Fan · Emma Wulfhorst · Eric Koester · Eric Miller · Eric Woo · Erica Ramon · Eytan Rubinstein · George Lubas · George Urbanik · Grace Guan · Grace Yeung · Hannah Goh · Hannah McNaughton · Henry Bitten · Henry Cobbs · Iftikhar Hussain · Ingrid Adams · Isabella Lovain · Isabella Siamundo · Iva Porfirova · Ivana Kafedjian · Jack Quigley · Jackson Fall · Jaclynn Rose · Jae Young Chang · Jakub Bereziewicz · James Harris · Jamie Manley · Janet Huang · Jared Kleinert · Jason Graig Hibono · Jay Murphy · Jennifer Anderson · Jennifer Ng · Jennifer Weltner · Jenny Jiang · Jerry Liang · Jessica Lavoie · Jo Tong · Joann Grabush · John Olear · Jordan Wolken · Jorge De La Cruz · Joseph Besgen · Joseph Meyer · Josh Ojo-Osagie · Joshua Castillon · Julie Aguirre · Karan Magu · Karen Davidson · Karin Klingaman · Kate Christensen · Katharina Eibel · Kathryn Besgen · Keara St.

Fort • Kimberly Alip • Kimberly Lu • Kirk Wei • Kirsten Spencer • Kris Cody • Krithika Kommana • Lauralei Singsank • Leah Novelli • Lillian Korinek • Linda Qin • Lisa Hanson • Lisa Randolph • Lisa Tsinis • Maddie Gatto • Madison Spinelli • Mahek Hooda • Mandy Lancour • Manthan Pakhawala • Marci Sorce • Marco Montalto Monella • Maria Marcelo • Marisa Mathias • Mariya Pugacheva • Mark Lubas • Masaki Kagesawa • Matthew Carp • Matthew Horesh Bernstein • Mauro Schenone • Maxwell Minsker • Megan Knyn • Meral Arik • Mia Moosbrugger • Mica Lagman • Michael Catelli • Michael Crawbuck • Michael Stromer • Michelle McGuigan • Miguel Santana • Molly Recker • Nadav Raichman • Nandaki Bonthu • Nardie Petisme • Natália Gieciová • Natasha Arya • Nathalie Naor • Navin Manglani • Neal Jean • Neha Dembla • Neyl Loukil-Borrás • Neyla Zniber • Nicholas Liao • Nicole Glucksman • Nicole Ng • Nisarg Patel • Nishanth Salinamakki • Noah Adams • Noah Skartvedt • Ole Marius Lervåg • Paulette Arnold • Peggy Wang • Pepper Lavoie • Peter Roland Petisme • Peyton Haag • Philip Ruffini • Priyanka Surio • Qiyuan Shengni • Rachel Alvarez • Rachel Dias • Rachel Kowal • Rachel Weintraub • Rachel White • Ralph Dalessandro • Raquel Baron • Ray Searles • Rebekah Horne • Rebekah Pedo • Reid Moncada • Rex Brown • Ria Swaminathan • Richa Jatia • Richard Branscomb • Richelle Yu • Riya Agrawal • Robert Tornu • Roberta Crockett • Ruchi Dhandhukia • Rushaunda Diaz • Ryan Borden • Sahitya Rajesh • Samantha Midwinter • Sandro Lubas • Sanjana Suraneni • Sarah Lubas • Sarah Yoon • Saransh Desai-Chowdhry • Sebastian Camacho • Sham Sarju • Shannon Lewis • Shannon Yu • Shaurya Sinha • Sheryl Dalal • Shreya Durbha • Shruti Manglik • Siena Mayer-Costa • Simmi Uppaladadium • Stein Bjelland • Stephanie Lay • Stephanie Zou • Steven Altman • Sunder Narayanan • Taylor Finley • Thais Groenen • Tiara Griffith • Tommy Ng • Tracyanne Haas • Urvashi Gupta • Valerie Shwalb • Victoria Kirby • Vincenzo De Santis • Wendy Ho • Wessel Torn • Whitney Dankworth • Zac Stern • Zachary Schwartz • Zawwar Khan • Zenia Pang

Continue the journey...

Visit www.youarewhereyougo.com/postcard to join the You Are Where You Go community by sharing your story of a travel experience that has shaped you into the person you are.

There you can also view Caitlyn's travel photography, author interviews, and more.

About the Author

Caitlyn Lubas's goal is to inspire a community of intentional, sustainably-minded travelers seeking authentic experiences and making the world a better place through increased cultural exchange.

Born in New Jersey to a Polish-Filipino-American family, Caitlyn became an avid traveler while attending college at NYU in New York City and beyond through six study abroad experiences across five continents. A high school valedictorian who got a dream job at Instagram – but then quit – Caitlyn chose to carve her own unique career path in the realm of travel and entrepreneurship just one year after graduating college. She currently embraces the life of a digital nomad and hopes one day to visit every country in the world.

9 781638 375425